Inequality, Poverty, and Neoliberal Governance

BROADVIEW ETHNOGRAPHIES & CASE STUDIES

URBAN SERIES | *editor: Rae Bridgman*

Inequality, Poverty, and

broadview press

Neoliberal Governance

ACTIVIST ETHNOGRAPHY IN THE
HOMELESS SHELTERING INDUSTRY

Vincent Lyon-Callo

Library and Archives Canada Cataloguing in Publication

Lyon-Callo, Vincent, 1964–
    Inequality, poverty, and neoliberal governance : activist ethnography in the homeless sheltering industry / Vincent Lyon-Callo.

Includes bibliographical references and index.
ISBN 1-55111-603-0

    1. Homelessness—United States.   2. Homelessness—Government policy—United States.
3. United States—Economic policy—1993–2001.   4. United States—Social policy—1993–
5. Shelters for the homeless—United States.   6. Poverty—United States.
7. Equality—United States.   I. Title.

HV4506.N67L96 2004   362.5'0973   C2004-904103-7

Broadview Press, Ltd. is an independent, international publishing house, incorporated in 1985. Broadview believes in shared ownership, both with its employees and with the general public; since the year 2000 Broadview shares have traded publicly on the Toronto Venture Exchange under the symbol BDP.

We welcome any comments and suggestions regarding any aspect of our publications— please feel free to contact us at the addresses below, or at broadview@broadviewpress.com / www.broadviewpress.com

North America
Post Office Box 1243,
Peterborough, Ontario,
Canada K9J 7H5
Tel: (705) 743-8990
Fax: (705) 743-8353
customerservice
  @broadviewpress.com

3576 California Road,
Orchard Park, New York
USA 14127

UK, Ireland, and
Continental Europe
NBN Plymbridge
Estover Road
Plymouth PL6 7PY
United Kingdom
Tel: +44 (0) 1752 202301
Fax: +44 (0) 1752 202331
Customer Service:
cservs@nbnplymbridge.com
orders@nbnplymbridge.com

Australia and New Zealand
UNIREPS
University of
New South Wales
Sydney, NSW, 2052
Tel: + 61 2 96640999
Fax: + 61 2 96645420
info.press@unsw.edu.au

Cover design and typeset by Zack Taylor, www.zacktaylor.com

This book is printed on 100% post-consumer recycled, ancient forest friendly paper.

Printed in Canada

Contents

Acknowledgements

This book is a much-revised version of work done as my dissertation at the University of Massachusetts/Amherst. Much of the research and the initial ideas explored more fully in this work were developed under the guidance of Jackie Urla, Enoch Page, John Cole, and Rick Wolff. I especially need to thank Enoch for being a consistent mentor as I struggled with rectifying my visions with the reality of anthropological practices. Art Keene, Julie Graham, Pat Greenfield, and Amy Harper all also provided valuable help during my time at UMass.

A slightly different version of Chapter Three appeared as "Medicalizing Homelessness: The Production of Self-Blame and Self-Governing within Homeless Shelters" (*Medical Anthropology Quarterly* 14(3): 328–45). An earlier version of part of the concluding chapter appeared as "Constraining Responses to Homelessness: An Ethnographic Exploration of the Impact of Funding Concerns on Resistance" (*Human Organization* 57(1): 1–8). Many of the ideas and examples covered in my article, "Homelessness, Employment, and Structural Violence: Exploring Constraints on Collective Mobilizations against Systemic Inequality," contained in *The New Poverty Studies: The Ethnography of Power, Politics, and Impoverished People in the United States*, edited by Judith Goode and Jeff Maskovsky (NYU Press, 2001), appear in this book. I am grateful to the many people who reviewed and contributed suggestions toward strengthening those ideas. Sue Hyatt, Judy Goode, Brett Williams, Karen Brodkin, and Jeff Maskovsky have been especially instrumental both in serving as models for how to do an engaged ethnography and in helping me develop and refine my arguments and writing.

I am also thankful for the advice and collegial approach to scholarship from other members of Society for the Anthropology of North America and the SUNTA Task Force on Poverty and Homelessness over the years. Many of the ideas presented in this book were first explored in their sessions at American Anthropological Association meetings. Rae Bridgeman and Irene Glasser from the task force as well as David Beriss have helped me to develop my thinking and practices for how to combine anthropology with anti-poverty activism. Additionally, Rae's comments on an earlier version of the manuscript were instrumental in making this into a readable work. I also want to thank Anne Brackenbury and the other members of the editorial team at Broadview Press for their assistance throughout the process.

Of course, none of this work would have been possible without the assistance and cooperation of many wonderful people in Northampton. It was a privilege to work with both my fellow staff members at the Grove Street Inn and the many advocates and activists throughout the community as well as getting to know the hundreds of people who happened to be homeless at various times during this work. I can only hope that I influenced them in ways that approach the positive impact they had on my life. I also have to thank Pam Hyman whose decision to hire me to work at the Operation Hope homeless shelter in Fairfield, Connecticut, in 1989 was instrumental in developing both my work and my self. Pam was a model for treating all people as deserving and worthy.

Finally, Sarah, Tobias, and Isabella Lyon-Callo have contributed to this work and to my life in immeasurable ways. I am thankful every day for their presence in my life.

Poverty and Homelessness

One warm October evening in 1996, I was in the driveway of a homeless shelter in Northampton, Massachusetts, shooting baskets with Domingo, a 17-year-old Puerto Rican man, who was preparing to try out for his high-school team. His girlfriend and a few other shelter residents were hanging out and commenting on our abilities. Our relatively tranquil evening was interrupted when another homeless man burst through the back door. John came waving a letter in his hand. "Can you believe this shit? Everyone got their letters today saying their checks are going to stop in January."

The letters John held were sent to people receiving social security disability payments as a result of a diagnosed substance-abuse disorder. As this was the only income for several people at the shelter, new legislation scheduled to eliminate it was a cause of great worry. A spirited discussion ensued about how many more people were going to become homeless because of these policy and welfare "reform" efforts. John argued, "if things don't change, there's going to be a revolution in this country soon."

Many of the people staying and working at this shelter agreed with John's sentiment. They articulated a belief that most people held misguided views about homeless people; but they maintained the liberal belief that if people were properly informed or once conditions became bad enough, these caring citizens would learn "the truth" and demand an end to homelessness. Of course, a few of the shelter residents argued that conservative social policies might continue, but John and most other staff, advocates, and homeless people were fairly certain that informed people would soon find the increasing levels of inequality and poverty unacceptable.

Several years have passed since that evening. Welfare "reform" has continued toward eliminating all vestiges of a social safety net (Fox Piven et al. 2002), while homelessness has become an even more routine feature of the nation. It is now "normal" for hundreds of thousands of people to have no housing. Even with what was widely proclaimed as an era of unprecedented wealth, prosperity, and economic growth coinciding with eight years of neoliberal efforts to provide services to "help" homeless people, homelessness and related indicators of inequality continued to increase throughout the late 1990s. For example, in 1999 the Department of Housing and Urban Development (HUD) along with other federal agencies released the most comprehensive study of homelessness in the United States demonstrating a pervasive homelessness problem throughout the nation (Interagency Council on the Homeless 1999). A few months later HUD released a further report suggesting that millions of additional American families were at risk for homelessness as 5.4 million families across the nation paid more than 50 per cent of their income for housing (US Department of Housing and Urban Development 2000). These reports confirmed the findings of several other studies (Burt 1997; Dolbeare 1999; National Coalition for the Homeless 1997; National Law Center on Homelessness and Poverty 1999; US Conference of Mayors 1998) in demonstrating increasing homelessness, hunger, housing stress, and inequality.

Yet the social movements and revolution forecast by John and others remain difficult to locate. Especially absent have been efforts of or with homeless people or shelter staff aimed at transforming cultural and political-economic conditions producing homelessness within vast wealth. This does not mean that governmental agencies and community members have not responded to homelessness. A massive amount of time and money is committed every year to address this issue, with little positive impact on actually decreasing homelessness. As these policies prove ineffectual in decreasing homelessness, citizens and elected officials throughout the country are increasingly turning to more punitive policies toward homeless people (Lyon-Callo 2001; National Law Center on Homelessness and Poverty 1999; Takahashi 1998).

Meanwhile, in many other cities, homelessness itself is no longer news. Many newspapers do not cover homelessness any longer except for stories during the winter holidays. Hunger and homelessness within general prosperity has become an ordinary and largely unchallenged part of life in the United States. How has that happened? How do we make sense of the lack of organized efforts such as those imagined by John? In this book I address these questions by drawing upon both my experiences of working in homeless shelters for much of the 1990s and over six years of ethnographic fieldwork studying the homeless sheltering industry in Northampton, Massachusetts. I argue that to understand homelessness we need to look at the combination of two factors. It is important to examine the impacts of neoliberal social and economic practices that have coincided with the rise of homelessness. Concurrently, we need to consider how people have, and have not, responded to this social restructuring in practice and what the effects of such practices have been. I begin with a brief overview of neoliberalism.

Neoliberalism, often promoted as more efficient government to help individuals and countries compete better, is both a return to classic liberalism's embracing of the private, "free" market as the solution to social problems and an embracing of the role of government to promote individualized competition and market-based policies. Neoliberalism is an embracing of privatization, marketization, and deregulation. This neoliberal restructuring has resulted in adjusted international trade polices, an increased globalization of capitalist production, and the promotion by international lending agencies of "structural adjustment" policies for much of the developing world. The structural adjustment policies promote both reductions in government spending on health, education, and social welfare programs and the privatization and deregulation of industries (Stiglitz 2002). The dominance of neoliberalism during the 1990s also led to similar policies within the United States. Privatization and deregulation in the name of efficiency and productivity have become the norm. Punishment and imprisonment have replaced many social programs, and those that remain, from public schools to social services, have a renewed focus on reforming individuals to better compete in "the free market" (Goode and Maskovsky 2001).

One result of neoliberal social policies has been growth in productivity and profitability. Accompanying that growth, however, are vastly increased global inequalities (Stiglitz 2002) with often violent consequences on the health and well-being of working people throughout the globe (Farmer 2003; Kim et al. 2000; Navarro 2000). Similar inequality has resulted within the United States as neoliberalism has produced great wealth for some, but poverty and homelessness for other people.

Neoliberalism, though, is more than just a set of practices and policies. Rather, it is a set of ideas and ways of imagining the world (Cruikshank 1996; Demartino 1999). Looking only at systemic conditions leaves many questions unanswered. We need to consider also the rhetorical justification for neoliberalism and how this has helped produce, and reproduce, social inequality. It is imperative to understand the material conditions, but it is also important to contemplate the discursive processes through which these conditions are accepted as a "normal" part of society. To demonstrate these points, let me turn more directly to the links between homeless policy and neoliberalism.

Neoliberal social welfare policy was given one of its first tests with homelessness. As the numbers of homeless people swelled during the early 1980s, an industry devoted to emergency shelters was developed. Over 3,500 new homeless shelters were opened throughout the nation between 1984 and 1988 (Jencks 1994: 15). As the numbers of homeless people grew, criticism of emergency shelters as the dominant public-policy response began to emerge during the early 1990s. Much of this criticism portrayed emergency shelters as largely unsafe warehouses doing little to address causes of homelessness (Anderson 1996; Gounis 1992).

Shortly after the start of Bill Clinton's first presidential term, public policies of all sorts began to embrace the neoliberal platform of market-based strategies and individualistic reforms of the Democratic Leadership Council.

Henry Cisneros, the new head of the US Department of Housing and Urban Development (HUD), pulled together a team of experts on homelessness to develop more effective approaches to the problem. Hoping to offer an alternative between warehousing people in emergency shelters and increasingly popular punitive responses, HUD and the Interagency Council on the Homeless unveiled the "continuum of care" (Interagency Council on the Homeless 1994).

The "continuum of care" plan was that communities throughout the country would facilitate private agencies' development of the services necessary to help homeless people and would manage those efforts through one integrated plan. It called for focused attention to address issues of mental health, physical health, and substance abuse. It emphasized the development of homeless people through privatized job training, education, and employment. The plan also called for additional resources needed to increase housing subsidies and to fight housing discrimination. Such an organized system of delivering services certainly would be an improvement over fragmented services. However, as the failure of the continuum of care to decrease homelessness should make clear by now, the problems causing homelessness lie not so much in how services are delivered, but rather in what the services do and do not do.

In practice, the continuum of care system became a neoliberal continuum only as a focus on individualized, market-based views of the social replaced the notion of a governmentally supported social safety net; however, funding for these programs was not forthcoming. Indeed, I suggest that the continuum of care was one of the earliest indicators of the Clinton administration's neoliberal bent. Support was not forthcoming for the articulated need for affordable housing units because such support came to be seen as potentially doing more harm than good. Providing housing to poor people was portrayed as increasing their dependence on government and decreasing their drive to become self-reliant individuals able to compete in the global market. This focus on market-based, individualized reforms of understood pathology within homeless people was strengthened with the election of George W. Bush, as evidenced by the plans outlined in a March 2003 report from the Department of Health and Human Services, "Ending Chronic Homelessness: Strategies for Action." The report called for more services to reform individual homeless people.

Many people obviously care about homelessness. But it has become "common sense" for that caring to take only the form of charity or services aimed at reforming homeless people. What I suggested in my conversation with John, and what I develop in this book, is that a hypothesis of individualized deviancy is at the root of contemporary responses to homelessness. This hypothesis suggests that the recent large-scale homelessness in the United

States is largely the result of deviance or pathology. A wide range of disorders is understood as contributing to making a person homeless, but these are all understood as being within the bodies or minds of individual people.

Basing my analysis on a long-term, activist, ethnographic engagement with the homeless sheltering industry in Northampton, Massachusetts (one of the cities which has most embraced the "continuum of care" approach), I trace the discursive impacts of the routine, well-meaning practices of social service workers, homeless people, advocates, and public officials as they attempt to resolve homelessness. While articulating rhetoric about links between inequality and homelessness, the actual shelter practices focus on helping homeless people cope with inequality. It seems that the goal is no longer to make society well through developing collective resistance strategies against social injustice, but rather to "normalize" the homelessness of individual homeless people. How did that happen? How have vast social inequality and widespread homelessness become acceptable? Why have the dominant responses to these cultural phenomena taken these particular forms? A desire to find answers to these questions was the motivation for the ethnographic methods and practices that I follow in this book as I attempt to shed some light upon the dynamics of the responses to homelessness in a neoliberal context.

Narrowly read, this is a book about homelessness in a small city in Massachusetts. More broadly, however, I am exploring the interrelationships between structural violence, social imaginings, discursive practices, and the possibilities of resistance under neoliberal governance. Drawing upon the example of Paul Farmer's (2003) work, I elucidate the workings of power and structural violence through ethnographic examples, with a focus on the material and discursive effects of neoliberal policies and practices. Although this is a study set in one city, it speaks more broadly as the policies and practices discussed are at the heart of the social welfare policies developed throughout the Clinton administration and expanded under the leadership of George W. Bush.

Why Northampton?

Most studies of homelessness and poverty in the United States focus on large, urban areas. Why then would a study of a small city of about 30,000 people nestled in the foothills of the Berkshire Mountains of Western Massachusetts be of any interest to anyone? What lessons might be learned from such a case study?

Northampton is an exemplary site for this research for a number of reasons. Perhaps most importantly, HUD's "continuum of care" concept has been embraced as the model through which hundreds of concerned and caring citizens in Northampton have responded to homelessness. This has resulted in vastly increased services for homeless people in substance abuse programs, mental health centers, and job training programs as local social service agencies have been greatly rewarded for what are seen as innovative programs that benefit those in the shelters.

Furthermore, as Tracey Kidder's book *Hometown* (1999) demonstrates, Northampton is recognized as a model of how to thrive despite deindustrialization. Northampton has managed to recover from the phenomenon of empty storefronts which has plagued nearby communities. With four elite colleges and the University of Massachusetts located close by, Northampton attracts many visitors. A busy Main Street full of art galleries, coffee shops, and upscale restaurants ends at the gates of Smith College. Avoiding the trend toward malls and national chains, the downtown area features locally owned movie theaters, bookstores, and a range of shopping options. A thriving arts and music community draws even more consumers to the city. The city also has a widespread reputation as a progressive and tolerant community through its well-publicized acceptance of a relatively large and open lesbian and gay population. In 1997, *Utne Reader* magazine declared Northampton to be Massachusetts' most enlightened town, while in 2001 *Outside* named it one of the ten best places to live.

Yet, beneath the surface, there is another side to the city. Like all of New England, Northampton has undergone significant economic restructuring in recent decades. One impact was the loss of 40 per cent of the manufacturing jobs in the county between 1980 and 1998. These were replaced largely by jobs in food service and retail trade. A 1999 study by the National Priorities Project found that 61 per cent of the jobs with the most growth in Massachusetts paid less than what the study defined as a living wage (National Priorities Project 1999).

As wages stagnated for many citizens, income inequality increased rapidly. When adjusted for inflation, the poorest 20 per cent of state residents saw their income decline by 2 per cent during this period while the wealthiest 20 per cent of the population experienced a 60-per-cent increase in income. This inequality has increased even more rapidly since 1980 with even the middle 20 per cent of the population seeing their incomes decline by 4 per cent while the incomes of the wealthiest 20 per cent increased by 18 per cent (Bernstein et al. 2000). At least in part as an outcome of these trends, many people are living on the margins of economic viability. A 1999 study by the Massachusetts Family Economic Self-Sufficiency Project found that an estimated 300,000 Massachusetts citizens (almost twenty-five per cent of the state's population) made too much money to qualify for federal assistance, but not enough to pay their bills.

Like many communities, Northampton also suffers from a lack of affordable housing units. As studies by HUD indicate, the availability of affordable housing has failed to keep up with requests for services nationally as the number of people on waiting lists for housing assistance continued to increase between 1996 and 1998, during the height of the economic boom (Department of Housing and Urban Development [HUD] 1999). According to the Bureau of Labor Statistics, rents increased faster than income for the 20 per cent of American households with the lowest incomes as the consumer price index for residential rent rose by 6.2 per cent between 1996 and 1998 (HUD 1999). In Northampton, the mean rent for a one-bedroom apartment was $706 in 1997, with an occupancy rate of over 95 per cent. Finally, the area is big enough to offer many social services, yet it is small and contained enough to provide an opportunity to know virtually all of the homeless individuals and service providers.

Analyzing Homelessness

My work illustrates how dominant industry practices produce both homeless subjects who aim to resolve homelessness through individual strategies of self-reform and shelter staff who are trained to manage homelessness and medicalize homeless people. Further, such practices produce social imaginings of deviant homeless people, thereby supporting neoliberal social policies. Such practices do little to address issues of systemic inequities such as increasing class exploitation, economic restructuring, and declining relative wages, all of which characterize the US in recent years.

There are a number of ways to understand how homelessness is produced while resistance to homelessness is constrained. As Marxist scholarship has demonstrated, careful attention needs to be paid to both the material and historical conditions that contribute to social inequality. Political and economic decisions regarding taxation policy, funding for housing, and international trade certainly have an impact upon people's lives. Overt economic domination through processes of class exploitation and rule by political entities plays a role in creating homelessness. Racial injustice, unequal educational opportunities, and gendered inequality are components of homelessness that are all fairly easy to document. However, as anthropological scholarship has established, poor people are active agents in their lives and there is little to be gained from understanding them as passive victims (Susser 1982; Gregory 1998; Goode and Maskovsky 2001). Instead, we need to investigate the apparent consent to the existence of homelessness.

One possible way of understanding consent is an argument that overt disciplining of people who resist inequality constrains the popularity of resistance. This likely has some impact. Even a cursory examination of recent history demonstrates that people who speak out and politically resist social inequalities risk being punished and putting their economic position in jeopardy. Direct and overt disciplining of people is all too real and clearly works to limit resistance both through policing from above and through fostering an atmosphere where people are afraid to put themselves at risk of losing any of their relative privilege. These processes have some impact on creating and perpetuating homelessness. Yet I argue that something much more insidious is also occurring.

It is my contention that many people have learned to comply with social inequality. The process of an unequal social order being culturally reproduced as "natural" (often without the use of overt domination or explicit coercion) is an example of hegemony. The process of hegemony refers to an organization of power and privilege taken for granted as "natural" and "common sense" (Williams 1977). Hegemony sets the conceptual parameters for the "reasonable" or "rational" understanding of and response to social circumstances. As Stuart Hall describes in his analysis of Thatcherism, hegemony functions so that "ruling ideas may dominate other conceptions of the social world by setting the limit to what will appear as rational, reasonable, credible, indeed sayable or thinkable, within the given vocabularies of motive and action available to us" (1988a: 44).

Hegemonic authority is often internalized as habits, understood as "common sense," and actualized in everyday practices: "In a quite literal sense, hegemony is habit forming" (Comaroff and Comaroff 1991: 23). Through the process of becoming "common sense," hegemonic understandings marginalize alternative understandings and actions. Thus, in order to understand routine practices and the formation of social policies it is imperative to examine the ideological resources people have available, from within their particular social milieu, in order to help them make sense of the conditions of their existence.

It is important to be mindful, however, of the subtlety of hegemony. Hegemony is never a matter of complete domination. To quote Raymond Williams, "the reality of any hegemony, in the extended political and cultural sense, is that, while by definition it is always dominant, it is never either total or exclusive" (1977: 113). As I will show with this account, neoliberal and medicalized thinking set the conceptual boundaries for the "realistic" or "reasonable" ways of responding to homelessness, but these dominant ways of knowing and being are challenged in a variety of ways. Sometimes these challenges take the form of alternative approaches or subterfuge, sometimes through coping strategies, and rarely through oppositional challenges.

Careful attention needs to be paid to the impact on any hegemony from such alternative or oppositional articulations and practices. As Williams suggests, "alternative political and cultural emphases, and the many forms of opposition and struggle, are important not only in themselves but as indicative features of what the hegemonic process has in practice had to work to control" (1977: 113). Hegemony is best understood not as static domination but rather as an ongoing process of establishing dominance. But how has the inequality resulting in homelessness become so dominant as to be "common sense"?

I argue that with homelessness the hegemony of a deviancy hypothesis supplements understandings about the "naturalness" of current economic and social relations to prevent homeless people and shelter staff from resisting homelessness through challenging structural inequality. I suggest that the concrete actions by which citizens and governments respond to homelessness are driven, at least in large measure, by images and understandings about homeless people and causes of homelessness. As homelessness has increased and become a fairly normal part of the nation's cultural landscape, most citizens have also developed "common sense" understandings about homeless people. Often this involves a stereotypical image of a substance-abusing homeless man or of a mentally ill homeless woman. Such views are cultivated through a combination of personal experience, anecdotal evidence, social-service remedies, and popular-culture representations about homeless people. As a result, people come to "know" homeless people as deviant or come to think of themselves as powerless to foster change. How concrete practices produce these conceptions of "the homeless" thus becomes an additional question needing further analysis.

Attention must then be paid to the discursive conditions under which homelessness is understood. The work of Michel Foucault (1991; 1979) and of scholars drawing on his work provides two crucial analytical tools for such an ethnographic analysis of homelessness. Foucault offers theoretical insights about how concrete actions produce the conceptual frameworks within which humans are made into subjects and how the processes of governmentality work together to produce hegemony. Contrary to a belief that an intentionally repressive project maintains social order, social inequality, and domination through ideological conditions mystifying "the truth" and creating compliance with the conditions creating homelessness, these scholars' work demonstrates how concrete practices and thoughts produce particular human subjects.

The work of scholars such as Nikolas Rose (1996a; 1996b), Ian Hacking (1995), and Barbara Cruikshank (1996) demonstrates how everyday, routine practices based upon particular historically produced conceptual understandings produce "reality" and "knowledge." In terms of poverty, everyday practices produce subjects such as "the poor," "the homeless," and "welfare mothers," resulting in particular understandings about both causes and treatments for these social problems. Once produced, these conceptualizations become the focus of governmental interventions aimed at neoliberal reform.

With the desire to reform "the poor" through governing, "the poor" have been constituted as subjects suffering from disorders of the self and in need of training and education to reform the characteristics and behaviors making them poor. On this view, the very bodies of poor people need to be regulated and reformed, leading to the development of government institutions, trained experts, and professional reformers like social workers, urban planners, teachers, health services, and police to "manage" and "regulate" the lives of "the poor" in the interest of "normalizing" them.

I argue in this text that similar dynamics have occurred in regard to "the homeless" and the development of the homeless sheltering industry. Concrete practices invent "the homeless" as a category of deviants requiring individualized treatment and reform. Discursive and material conditions limit the range of permissible understandings and activities of both homeless people and people working in the shelters. These responses to homelessness are manifestations of what Foucault referred to as governmental techniques.

Nikolas Rose summarizes the Foucauldian concept of governmentality as follows: "government is a way of conceptualizing all those more or less rationalized programs, strategies, and tactics for the 'conduct of conduct,' for acting upon the actions of others in order to achieve certain ends" (1996a: 12). Governance acts as a technique for "making up and acting upon a population and its constituents to ensure good and avert ill" (Rose 1996a: 322). But government is not "just acting upon the actions of others." People have developed techniques both to govern other people and to govern themselves. In this light, governance can be seen not simply as something imposed from above, but as including both the social actors doing the governing and those being governed.

Maintaining social order and social inequality by force is less desirable than a well-tempered social regulation. As Paul Rabinow has argued, "implicit in the technologies of governmentality was the notion that it was possible to transform society so that both force and politics would become unnecessary" (1989: 232). Clearly, this has never worked out completely as force and politics remain necessary to quell unrest at various moments, but, as I will demonstrate with homelessness, people are often ruled by how they learn to think of "the homeless," their selves, and their place in the world.

Homeless people and shelter staff are often ensnared within the material and discursive webs of capitalism and the welfare state. They respond to the eruption of homelessness throughout the nation in a variety of ways: sometimes in open defiance, but more often through more personal strategies of coping and accommodating. In many cases these very strategies contribute to the maintenance of homeless discipline and control. Everyday practices enacted by homeless people and by shelter staff allow them to "escape [domination] without leaving it" (de Certeau 1984: xiii). Homelessness and the "natural" processes of social inequality remain largely unchallenged as everyday practices focus on reforming homeless people and developing coping strategies. In this work, I demonstrate how the very practices operating within the shelters contribute to the production of docile and deviant bodies. Practices intended to resolve homelessness contribute to its maintenance.

Research Methods

Although becoming slightly more accepted, anthropological studies situated within North America remain marginalized within the discipline. As a few anthropologists have begun to work within North America recently, much of the initial research has focused on "social problems" in the United States, including "the homeless." Many contemporary ethnographic studies in the United States have roots in anthropological work produced in the 1960s and 1970s that focused almost exclusively on the most downtrodden and "exotic" of poor African Americans who were often marginal even within their own communities. Such studies neglected the scores of hard-working people struggling in these communities and often failed to contextualize the subjects within an analysis of systemic inequality (Hyatt 1995). That focus remains in much ethnographic work today as problems are often treated as evidence of pathologies, disorders, or aberrations. As Robin Kelley (1997) argues, many ethnographers actually help to construct dominant imaginings through their focus on "subcultures," reinforcing and reifying culturally constructed differences and producing support for particular social policy.

Ethnographic work focusing only on "the poor" or "the homeless" miss interconnections between social actors. Similarly, these ethnographic studies also neglect the discursive processes producing "the homeless" or "the ghetto" as cases to be managed or governed. Similar dynamics sometimes continue today as demonstrated by Philippe Bourgois's award-winning work *In Search of Respect: Selling Crack in El Barrio* (1995). Bourgois admits that the crack dealers he studies are in the clear minority within their own community. Yet they are virtually the exclusive focus of his study. I am not arguing that such texts are not informative or useful in many ways. Bourgois's book provides a compelling, first-hand examination of a part of the United States that most people know only through popular media constructs. What I am suggesting is that anthropologists can be more aware of the potential impact of their studies and reflective about how they can function. In light of these concerns, I made the tactical decision to focus my study not on "the homeless" or simply to provide another ethnographic description of behaviors of homeless people. Instead, I study homelessness by looking at interconnections between homeless and housed people through a focus on the homeless sheltering industry.

I worked within the sheltering industry for most of the 1990s. Working in shelters in Connecticut and Massachusetts prior to and during my graduate school years both transformed how I thought about homelessness and people who happened to be homeless and provoked many questions that I wanted to investigate. In that work, I became increasingly frustrated by what I saw as a seeming acceptance and normalization of fairly widespread homelessness despite the wealth in the communities where I was working. Deciding that an ethnographic account would allow for the most detailed, thorough method for exploring my questions about that seeming acceptance and about how issues of poverty and inequality seemed to be transformed into issues of individual pathology, I started ethnographic research in the early 1990s.

My ethnographic work focuses predominantly on the lives of shelter staff, homeless people, shelter administrators, and local advocates over a six-year period. This population represents a cross-section of those involved with the homeless industry, reflecting a variety of experiences, educational levels, and positions in the community to investigate the analytical categories and social systems. I explore everyday practices interacting with the discursive and material conditions that produce homelessness. In this way, I build upon the work on homelessness recently done by Talmadge Wright (1997) and Deb Connolly (2000) demonstrating that homeless people are active social agents.

During most of the time I was engaged in this research, I was employed 30–50 hours per week at the Grove Street Inn, a 20-bed emergency shelter for homeless men and women in Northampton. Being at the shelter for six years allowed me to participate in daily shelter routines. I spent thousands of hours ethnographically detailing how homeless people, shelter staff, local advocates, and local policy makers responded to homelessness. I participated in a broad range of activities including weekly staff meetings, case management sessions, the daily enforcement of shelter rules, statistical record keeping, the development of shelter policies, intake procedures, efforts to locate housing and income, the development of grant applications, and staff training. Additionally, I participated in an array of community-based activities and community forums on homelessness, including an ongoing engagement with a community group consisting of local service providers, clergy, volunteers, city officials, business owners, and other community members seeking a long-term approach to homelessness. Data from these activities were supplemented by a series of open-ended interviews with nine staff members, several dozen homeless people, shelter administrators, local advocates, and local policy makers. I also compiled statistical data on over 500 individuals who stayed at the shelter between January 1994 and December 1996. In all of this work, I looked at not only on what people said, but on what they did, focusing much attention on the effects of routine, everyday practices through which people responded to homelessness. Specific people discussed in the study consented to participate and their names were changed in the text. Interviews and meetings discussed in the text were most often taped, but a few conversations were reconstructed after I arrived home from the shelter on that particular day.

A note about possible ethical conflicts in doing this type of research must be added. I worked as a staff member in roles including assistant director of the shelter during much of this research. Clearly, in that position, I had potential power over people both working at and living at the shelter. Therefore it was imperative that, while I engaged in dialogue with people, I not impose my opinions upon them or coerce anyone into embracing my notions. With the staff this was relatively easy as we ran the shelter through formal consensus in a non-hierarchical manner where positions such as director became positions of increased responsibility and not necessarily power over other staff members. Hiring decisions were also made in a collective, consensual manner. With respect to people staying at the shelter, my level of engagement with them varied from person to person. For many poor people, homelessness is a temporary, although perhaps recurring, event. Dozens of people stayed at the shelter for only a night or two. Likewise, there clearly were dozens of people who were in no position to engage in debates with me. The people staying at the shelter who are discussed in detail in this text, therefore, are a select group of people whom I came to know quite well over a relatively long period of time. As we came to know one another, we engaged in discussions about a whole range of topics. Some of those discussions are covered here. Finally, no private, confidential discussions, counseling sessions, case management discussions, or issues of supervision of staff or guests were used in the ethnography.

An Engaged, Activist Ethnography

In my work in Northampton, I analyzed how the everyday practices within the shelter served to medicalize homelessness, produce particular modes of governance and subject positions, and constrain the possibilities of collective mobilizations. But what was I to do then? Is it enough for anthropologists to gather their data and do their analysis for the sake of simply producing new knowledge for others to utilize? Finding such a stance ethically troubling as well as believing that it would be impossible to accomplish in practice, I instead drew upon the recent calls for a politically engaged ethnography and employed an explicitly activist methodology.

Although it has by no means become the dominant trend within anthropology, there has been much talk in recent years of the potential for a more engaged anthropology. What scholars mean by engagement, however, ranges broadly. Some want anthropologists to write and speak in ways and places that are more accessible to the general population. The hope is that anthropological insights could influence public opinions and more people might understand the relevance of anthropology to the world around them. Another possibility is doing ethnographic work such as that done by Anna Lou Dehavanon (1993, for example), where the focus is to provide information to "policy makers" with a view to influencing the direction of public policy. It certainly would not hurt to develop means for sharing ethnographic findings more broadly. However, public officials are likely to ignore anthropological knowledge unless it becomes politically expedient not to do so through our working to transform common sense understandings.

A more compelling type of engaged ethnography is exemplified by the work of Pem Buck Davidson (2001) and Paul Farmer (2003). Writing in an accessible style, they analyze the shortcomings of liberal helping efforts, the dynamics by which poor and working class people are exploited and marginalized, and how poor people appear to consent to their oppression. Reading such ethnographic work provides clear clues to both understanding and working against oppression and structural violence.

What I am suggesting, however, is a slightly different type of scholarship. Building upon the community-based participatory action research advocated by Merrill Singer (1990) and Jean and Stephen Schensul (1978), I practice an explicitly interventionist and activist ethnographic method. This is not, however, simply advocacy for a particular political stance or position. Rather, drawing upon Faye Harrison's (1991) argument that to fully decolonize anthropology we must go beyond rethinking how we write ethnography and instead problematize the ethnographic relationship through working with people in a more equitable, collaborative manner, I engaged in a constantly evolving dialogue with community members. The goal was not simply to find data to support my views, nor was it my intention to impose my views upon people. I am certainly not advocating an ethnography where the ethnographer comes in as an expert who knows the "truth" and can prescribe "solutions." I am also not suggesting a methodology where "experts" enlighten through teaching the misinformed what to do and think for their own good. The world already has more than enough of those people; indeed, when I first began to work in homeless shelters, I know I tried helping homeless people with just such missionary zealousness. My work gradually changed, however, to challenging common sense understanding by engaging in dialogue.

As Akhil Gupta and James Ferguson (1997) have argued, an activist ethnography that simply associates the research with a particular political stance remains problematic in that it still positions the anthropologist as occupying an external and privileged position. Instead, they advocate an activist ethnography "as a way of pursuing specific political aims while simultaneously seeking lines of common political purpose with allies who stand elsewhere." I agree with them, but, closer still to the method I employed is what Merrill Singer and his colleagues describe as "community centered praxis" (1992). Singer et al. argue that if ethnographers really want to intervene in the problems they study, they need to work closely with community members as colleagues. The research of Cheryl Rodriguez in Florida (2003) and Dana-Ain Davis in New York (2003) epitomizes the type of activist, engaged scholarship I carried out in the study.

If we want to transform inequalities, we cannot maintain the hierarchical stance of the neutral, detached, impartial observer. I suggest that not only is such an approach impossible to maintain, but attempting it would also have decreased the willingness of people to take part in the study. As one shelter worker, Ann, told me, "Are you going to write a paper or get some real work done?" She made it quite clear that, if I was not going to commit fully to engaging in the struggle with her and the other staff and homeless people, she would participate in my study on only a very cursory level. Not everyone articulated this sentiment so clearly, but it was a recurring theme. When people saw me as an advocate and ally, then the ethnographic notes and interviews became a welcome diversion and just part of my commitment to our shared struggle rather than an unwelcome intrusion. Of course, working as a colleague does not eliminate power differentials, but, perhaps even more importantly, people allowed me access to thoughts and actions that would otherwise have remained hidden. I worked with people in all facets of their struggles. I worked as an active agent with the people I was ethnographically studying and served as an advocate for many individuals. Fundamental to my ethnography is that I did not work only as a colleague, but I also engaged in dialogue with them in an effort to problematize routine, everyday discourse and practices. I agree with Nancy Scheper-Hughes' point that a politically engaged ethnography does not simply mean trying to make everyone like you, but rather developing relationships of mutual trust and respect so that we "enter freely into dialogues—and sometimes into conflicts and disagreements—with my teachers, challenging them on views just as they challenge me on mine" (1992). When my analysis led me to understand that normal helping practices were doing very little to decrease homelessness, I shared my critiques with a range of people. My goal was to help produce more talk, more reflection, and possibly new understandings and practices to emerge through dialogue about the effects of routine practices. However, I did this through engaging in open, respectful exchanges with people who came to regard me as a colleague and ally through years of working together. We may have disagreed at various times, but we maintained a high level of mutual respect.

As I mentioned above, I did not tell people what they should do or think. There were actually many times when a staff member or a homeless person would become frustrated with me for not doing so. They would argue that I needed to ask fewer questions and give more answers, since I was the one with the education on the issue. My answer was that homelessness is a complex social phenomenon and that it would be arrogant to presume that I could simply point out the correct path for all to follow. More important, though, is that doing so would have fundamentally undermined my aim of fostering more democracy, more freedom, and more equality through my work. Therefore, I agree with Gupta and Ferguson (1997) that the political task is not to "share" knowledge with those who lack it, but to forge links between different forms of knowledge that are possible from different locations and to trace lines of possible alliance and common purpose between them.

Conducting publicly and politically engaged research has the potential to help produce new, potentially transformative thinking and practice in local communities. However, perhaps an equally important benefit from doing activist, dialogically engaged ethnography is the new knowledge and insights that become possible. It was only through engaging in open and honest dialogues, debates, and, at times, disagreements with homeless people, shelter staff, administrators, elected officials, and advocates that the full range of both material and discursive constraints on collective mobilization, as well as the potential for collaborative resistance against structural violence, became clear.

I would advocate this type of ethnography only after developing strong bonds with people through a lengthy period of working with them. However, the consequences of not doing engaging in an activist fashion would be almost to perpetuate the structural violence I saw every day. Would it be better to remain "neutral" and not raise the fact that it had somehow become routine for the staff at the shelter to turn away people every night or to provoke dialogue about the issue in the hope that a new possibility might emerge out of our collective effort? I chose the second option: taking the risk of acting, but doing so by prefacing my efforts with a clear indication that I did not have the answers but rather wanted to work toward new understandings collectively. The following chapters lay out some of the partial answers I developed based upon my unique position as both ethnographer and staff member and outlines the new practices that emerged through this work.

CHAPTER 1

The Political-Economic Context

There has been a large increase in the number of people living on the streets or in homeless shelters throughout the United States since the late 1970s. On the most basic level, homelessness can be seen as a matter of income and availability of "affordable housing." In this chapter, I articulate a theoretical framework for examining the recent increase in homelessness by posing two classic Marxist questions: What are the political-economic conditions causing homelessness and who benefits from these conditions?

To some traditional Marxists wedded to economic determinism, the answers to these questions might appear self-evident. An argument could be put forth that homelessness is simply a result of changing material conditions such as deindustrialization, the increased globalization of capital and production, a changed income tax structure over the last two decades, a decreased commitment to building affordable housing, and the decreased strength of unions. Many citizens simply cannot afford to secure housing due to the increased levels of exploitation resulting from these changing material conditions. Clearly, the wealthy and powerful benefit. The ideologies supporting such domination by capital are examples of false consciousness masking the "true" conditions. Average citizens are duped into "false" beliefs determined by the dominant material conditions. As Stuart Hall has stated, this type of deterministic, structural Marxism might best be characterized as "a theory of the obvious. The question delivers no new knowledge, only the answer we already knew. It's a kind of a game-political theory as a Trivial Pursuit. In fact, the reason we need to ask the question is because we really don't know" (1988b: 165).

I suggest posing the questions above in a slightly different way. Yes, it is imperative that we analyze material conditions. But it is also important for an analysis to contemplate the discursive processes through which conditions are accepted as a "normal" part of our society and how these make sense to people at precise historical moments.

A Flourishing National Economy: What About Homelessness?

Much has been written about the changing local and global economy. Many manufacturing plants in the Northeast and Midwest were shut down as production work was transferred to lower waged areas in Asia, the Southeast US, and Central America. The development of new technologies, more efficient production processes, and new means of transportation all played a role. Additionally, corporate mergers, an increase in the economic power of global conglomerates, creation of part-time "homework" throughout the globe, and a growth in the temporary labor industry within the US occurred. Corporate downsizing, often despite increased productivity and efficiency, further resulted in decreased employment options. The combination of well-paying manufacturing jobs being replaced by non-unionized, less stable employment in the service industries with gentrification in the name of community development (Williams 1996: Marcuse 1989) contributed to an increase in inequality and homelessness over the last two decades (Burt 1992; Hopper et al. 1985; Wolch and Dear 1993).

Changes in tax codes enacted throughout this period also played a contributing role in the rise of economic inequality throughout the US. For example, the highest marginal income tax rate in the United States was cut from 70 per cent in 1980 to 39.6 per cent in 1996 (Friedman 1997: 23). Likewise, the percentage of federal tax revenue from corporate taxes decreased from 23 per cent in 1960 to 10 per cent in 1995 (Albelda et al. 1996: 21).

One result of the social and political-economic changes has been a sharply increased redistribution of resources toward the wealthiest members of the society. Studies by the Center on Budget and Policy Priorities (1994) and the Center for Popular Economics (Albelda et al. 1996) found the wealthiest people in the United States became much wealthier over the last twenty years while the poorest have become relatively worse off. The absolute number of people living in poverty has increased and the relative share of the national wealth possessed by the poorest 40 per cent of the population has decreased even as the national economy has produced more absolute wealth.

The distribution of aggregate household income in the US documents the trend toward increased inequality. In 1993, the wealthiest 5 per cent of the population received 20 per cent of the nation's total income while the poorest 40 per cent received only 12.7 per cent. Twenty years earlier the distribution was 16.6 per cent for the top 5 per cent and 14.7 per cent for the lowest 40 per cent of families (Center on Budget and Policy Priorities 1994: 57). This trend has continued in recent years. According to Census Bureau data, real median income in 1995 fell to 3.8 per cent below that of 1989 (US Bureau of the Census 1996).

Increasing inequality becomes even more significant when considering how the share of national wealth increased for the wealthiest members of the society while decreasing for the working poor. The share of national income going to the top fifth of all households (49.1 per cent) in 1994 was the highest proportion recorded up to that point, and the share of national income going to the bottom fifth of households (3.6 per cent) was the lowest (National

Coalition for the Homeless 1997). Data from the US Department of Labor demonstrate that, after adjustment for inflation, average hourly wages paid to non-supervisory workers were lower in 1993 and 1994 than in any years since 1964 (Lav and Lazere 1996: 5).

However, an increasingly unequal distribution of wealth and resources cannot, by itself, account for the growth of homelessness. We also need to consider the cost and availability of housing when contemplating why increased poverty took the particular form of homelessness. As poverty has increased, restructuring has occurred in the funding of social services and social welfare programs. The declining role of the federal and state governments in funding housing programs has certainly contributed to the recent increase in the number of homeless people on the streets of the nation.

As discussed in the introduction, several studies have examined the structural processes that have resulted in the nation's low-income housing crisis (Interagency Council on the Homeless 1999; National Law Center on Homelessness and Poverty 1999; Dolbeare 1999; Lazere 1995; Burt 1997; Jenks 1994; Interagency Council on the Homeless 1999; O'Flaherty 1996; US Conference of Mayors 1998). HUD (2000) suggested this was due to a strong economy leading to higher rents, a lack of governmental support for adequate section 8 subsidies, and a decrease in both public and private housing stock. As a result, 26 per cent of requests for emergency shelter nationwide were unmet due to a lack of shelter space in 1998 (US Conference of Mayors 1998).

The recent national shortage of affordable housing has not always been the case. In 1970, after several years of increased government expenditures on housing, the 7.4 million low-cost rental units in the US represented an abundance of 900,000 more units than the number of low-income renters (6.5 million). In 1973, there were 5.1 million non-subsidized rental units with costs of $300 per month or less (in 1993 dollars). By 1993, this situation had been reversed. The number of low rent units fell to 6.5 million (only 2.9 million of which were non-subsidized), while the number of low-income potential renters increased to 11.2 million. A shortage of 4.7 million units was the result (Lazere 1995: 2). This trend increased throughout the 1990s as the number of affordable units fell to 4.9 million by 1999 (National Coalition for the Homeless 2003). The result has been long waiting lists for housing assistance, tenants paying over 50 per cent of their income toward rent, and homelessness.

The Hidden Side of Northampton: Poverty, Inequality, and Homelessness

As homelessness has increased throughout the nation, people are finding it increasingly difficult to access services (even a shelter bed) and to locate income adequate to maintain housing. In Northampton, approximately 200 people stayed at the Grove Street Inn between 1994 and 1996, but less than 20 per cent moved into non-sheltered housing. This entire region's economy witnessed major structural changes, resulting in job losses especially for "unskilled" and "low skilled" workers (Market Street Research 1994: 12). The overall poverty levels in the city and region increased consistently during the 1980s and 1990s. However, the cost of housing remains high.

Homelessness was barely visible in the Northampton area before the mid-1980s. The occasional homeless person was sheltered through a small, church-run program and a family shelter. This changed dramatically during the 1990s with a rather dramatic increase in homeless shelters, services, and the demand for beds. Prior to 1994, the shelter where this research is focused was able to provide for all those seeking a bed, but by 1995 it became routine to turn people away. The shelter maintained a waiting list of over 40 people throughout 1995 and 1996 despite the inception of two newer programs in the city. The vast majority of people on the waiting list for shelter never obtain a bed. During 1995, 193 different people stayed at the shelter while 199 other people attempted to enter but were turned away because of a lack of beds.

Once a homeless person finally makes it into the shelter, relaxation and regrouping are not an option. Their attention must quickly turn to a plan for leaving. However, less than one-third of the people who stayed between 1994 and 1996 moved into permanent housing after leaving. Many left town, moved to a different shelter, moved to some treatment program, lived in the woods surrounding the city, or doubled up with family and friends. In fact, only four people staying at the shelter during 1995 were able to rent an apartment (not including rooming house rooms) in Northampton. Additionally, many of those who do move out of the shelter eventually try to return. During 1995, for example, fifty-four of the people staying at the shelter had stayed there previously.

Let me try to explain some of the difficulties confronting people in Northampton by relating the experiences of homeless people. Jonathan, a man in his early 20s, stayed at the shelter during the autumn and winter of 1993 and 1994. He had come to the area hoping to attend the University of Massachusetts. As a bright and articulate young, white man, he was quickly able to secure employment while trying to save money for housing and school. He was a model guest during both of his stays, rarely broke any shelter rules, and frequently helped to insightfully mediate disputes between guests around the shelter. Despite his efforts, he was never able to afford housing in the city.

During his first stay, Jonathan worked as a cashier in a local supermarket and conducted telephone surveys. In 1994, he found a job washing dishes in an upscale local restaurant. Both times the shelter staff were supportive of his efforts, extended his stays, and suggested all they could think of for locating housing. The wages paid in the service work available were just not enough, however, to secure housing.

Jonathan and I discussed his plans one evening. He had been working for two months washing dishes five nights a week. For almost two months he had been looking for an apartment with another shelter resident, Tom, who worked with him in the restaurant. They wanted to avoid living in rooming houses and had been saving their money for an apartment.

That night, Jonathan told me that he was planning to move to South Carolina to find lower rents: "I can get an apartment for half-price there during the off-season."

I asked about pay and he said that they pay the same thing as the Northampton area: "They pay you $5 an hour wherever you go to wash dishes if you do a good job and get in at a good restaurant. I just need to get out of this town."

Jonathan and Tom had been trying to find a shared living situation with two co-workers. They searched everywhere for potential housing to no avail. They soon found that they were ineligible for any assistance that did not entail waiting lists several years long. His solution was to leave town, give up on school, and try to locate housing where he envisioned less costly rents. As he put it, "minimum wage is just about the same everywhere."

Jonathan, like several other homeless people I've known, placed much of the blame for his inability to find housing on preferential treatment for students, "minorities," and the "disabled." He stated, "They [the shelter staff and local politicians] don't want to help anybody in this town unless they're lesbian or Puerto Rican. These people just want to get a check. It takes about two minutes to get a job in this town if you want one. They [minorities] just don't want to work and they get all the help." His individualized strategy of trying to work his way out of homelessness through being a responsible, hard-working person proved unsuccessful. Staff and local policy makers had little to offer the working homeless like Jonathan as the shelter case management and city programs all focused on treating disorders within homeless people, not addressing issues of wages or housing cost. To some extent, it is hardly surprising that Jonathan turned to blaming other poor people and "the government" when his individualized strategy of working for wages failed to end his homelessness. No discursive alternatives for understanding homelessness were made available to him.

One night I asked Jonathan if he had tried to get any assistance from the shelter staff. He responded, "What are they going to do for me? Are they going to get me a place to live? They're just for helping crazy people or people get a check or a room in a rooming house. I have a job. There's just no housing you can afford in this place. Everywhere that might be cheap enough is either a shitty place to live or has a huge waiting list. Plus, they always want to rent to college students. I don't want to live in one of those rooming houses on Pleasant Street. I'd rather camp outside. I work hard and should be able to have a decent place to live."

At another point during the evening he mentioned that his bosses were trying to convince them to remain in Northampton. "They're trying to get us to stay, but there's nothing they can do. This town hates homeless people. Everywhere else I've been people are more willing to help you. Some places people even help without you asking. Here they just don't want to see you."

Vin: "Well there does seem to be something your bosses can do. They could pay you enough to live on."

Jonathan: "Yeah, they could give me 40 hours every week, but I still won't be able to afford an apartment"

Vin: "But how about paying you $7 an hour instead of $5?"

Jonathan: "They can't do that. They won't stay in business."

Jonathan could not envision his food-service job paying a decent wage. Like many other people, Jonathan accepts as natural that such jobs must remain low paying and that decisions about distribution of the surplus naturally are the province of the employer. The possibility that food-service jobs can become "good" jobs remains unimaginable. At the very least, he feels powerless to change the pay in these jobs.

Later that night, I was watching the evening news on television with Jonathan and four other homeless people. A short story came on the news about some local college students who were going to learn about homelessness by sleeping outside for a night. The spokeswoman for the group said that it was better than just giving money to a shelter because, with this experience, these students will now realize what it's really like being homeless. The news story did not go over too well in the shelter.

Jonathan: "Look at those assholes. Oh yeah, sleeping outside in a big group on your college campus is going to teach you a lot. Why don't they sleep out by themself in a cardboard box under a bridge down by the river. Look at those sleeping bags they have. What homeless person can afford a sleeping bag like that?"

Wayne: "Yeah, why don't they sleep in the city where a cop will come by and kick the shit out of them when they fall asleep?"

Jonathan: "They're having a fucking camp out. Look, they have cookies with them and are playing cards."

Vin: "I bet they had dinner in the cafeteria before they came outside."

Jonathan: "And they have breakfast waiting for them. Why don't they see what it's like to not have any food and not be able to sleep without worrying about being beaten up or robbed? They just want to feel good about themselves. How are they going to help me get a room I can afford by camping out together?"

Jonathan was quite articulate in criticizing minorities, local shop owners, landlords, and the children of the privileged. He argued that they contributed to his homelessness in Northampton. Yet he could not conceive of any collective strategies for altering those conditions. His efforts remained on the level of an individual trying to obtain housing through hard work.

A few weeks later, several of the shelter staff and guests attended a conference on homelessness sponsored by the US Department of Health and Human Services. The conference, organized primarily by Phillip Mangano (who later moved on to head the delivery of homeless services for the Bush administration), was designed to get service providers and homeless individuals to outline gaps in the continuum of care system. Health and Human Services annually allocated millions of dollars throughout Massachusetts and this conference was developed as a strategy for getting that money.

I came by the shelter to meet people going to the conference. Two staff members were recruiting people to go and they asked Tom and Jonathan.

Jonathan responded, "I can't waste my time with that. I'll still be homeless when I get home. They don't care what I think and they're not going to do anything about homelessness."

Tom joined in: "But, you guys go and who knows, maybe something will happen, but it won't help me."

I responded: "Maybe, you're right. There aren't any [benefits for the working poor] because it's thought that you must somehow deserve being homeless. It must be your fault, but these are the people who design the programs and it's a chance to have them hear your story."

Jonathan: "Maybe it is my fault. Maybe I'm crazy too. I'm here aren't I?"

Except for his self-condemnation, Jonathan's analysis turned out to be fairly accurate. Three people from the shelter attended the conference with us. They appeared to be the only homeless people there. Hundreds of experts (shelter staff, academics, city planners, politicians, and advocates) spent the day discussing how their programs helped homeless people and all of the wonderful work they could with more money. Virtually all discussions focused on how to fix homeless individuals. The most clearly articulated assumption was that most homeless people were disabled and needed expert help. The call for funding was intended to subsidize professional help through treatment and transitional programs. There was no examination of housing cost or wages paid.

Finally, Jonathan did leave Northampton and headed south hoping to find housing. Like ten per cent of people staying at the shelter during 1994–96, he decided that the only solution to his problem was to leave Northampton and hope for better luck somewhere else. He wanted to improve his income potential and job skills through education, but he couldn't afford college. He worked hard but became frustrated by his inability to afford decent housing. Feeling that he was powerless to alter the wages paid locally, the cost of housing, or any systemic conditions, he "chose" to leave town and try his luck elsewhere. The shelter staff and local policy makers could offer Jonathan no substantial assistance. As the following sections will demonstrate, Jonathan's experience is far from unique.

WORKING YOUR WAY OUT OF HOMELESSNESS?

One evening, Jerry, a 24-year-old white man, came back quite irate to the shelter from work as a cashier at the local Stop and Shop supermarket. He sat down in the shelter's living room and began to complain about his job.

Jerry: "They're screwing me out of my raise. I was supposed to get my six-month raise last week, but they said that I already got the raise when the minimum wage was raised in January and I'm not going to get my year raise either because they say that I'll get that raise in October when the minimum wage increases again."

Aaron (a newer staff): "But, you are getting a raise."

Jerry: "No, I'm getting minimum wage still and I'll still be getting minimum wage even after working there a year. I'll make the same pay as someone who was hired that day after I've been working there for a year. I wasn't given a raise. It was mandated by the state. I won't get a six-month or a year raise and all the union says is that Stop and Shop can't afford it."

Vin: "Right, Stop and Shop can't afford it if they want to keep their profits at the extraordinary level they are at."

Jerry: "It's bullshit. They must make a million dollars a month in the Hadley store alone. On a good day, I take in over $10,000 in one six-hour cashier shift and they usually have 15 registers going at once."

Vin: "Of course there are other costs like shipping and stocking, but they say they can only afford to pay you $30 for a shift in which you bring in around $10,000. They say they can't afford it, but did you know that Stop and Shop was just bought out by a bigger company last week. Their shares increased from about $3 when they bought the company in 1983 to something like $39 a share now and they say that they can't afford to pay their workers a living wage."

Jerry's response to the sale of Stop and Shop was one of great skepticism about it improving his work conditions at all. "Yeah, I think it was a Danish company. What they're saying at work is that they'll probably lay some people off. They just spent a lot of money on buying the company and they need to keep profits up. They'll probably raise prices, lower the price of scan saver items, and lay some people off."

Vin: "The union is too weak to do anything about it?"

Jerry: "They can't fight it. Most of the people who work there are part-time. They hire a lot of high-school and college students and housewives or retired people. There aren't too many of us who have to support ourselves from working there. We can't speak up. We need the job."

Vin: "Even if you can't afford a place from the pay and hours they give you?"

Jerry: "It's better than nothing. At least I have a job. It's like I say. It's easy to get a part-time job in this town. Anyone can get one, but you can't support yourself on it."

Vin: "And they won't give you full-time work."

Jerry: "You have to work there for years to work full-time."

Vin: "Even if they gave you 40 hours, you couldn't afford to live on it in this town. Think about it. Even with working there full-time, you'll take home about $170 a week. That comes out to $680 a month. Where can you find an apartment in Northampton for less than $550 which leaves you nothing for food, clothes, transportation, or heat."

Jerry: "That's another thing. They won't give you a set schedule either. Last week, I work starting at 8 in the morning, but this week it's at 10:30. Your schedule changes each week so you can't do any of your own business. You can't even schedule a doctor's appointment for the next week because you never know when you have to work."

Vin: "Never mind trying to get a second part-time job. You couldn't possibly hold it because neither one will give you set hours."

Jerry: "It's just shit. If this was the 1950s I wouldn't be homeless. My father graduated from high school and got a job right away in doing tool and dye work. They gave him good pay and benefits and on the job training. There just aren't good jobs like that anymore."

Vin: "I was just looking at some statistics on this the other day and the county has lost over half its manufacturing jobs in the last fifteen years."

Jerry: "That's why I'm stuck in this job. I'm 23 years old, have been in the military, and can't support myself. The only jobs where young people can support themselves on in this town are ones where they know someone or where their parents get them the good job."

Vin: "I think that something you said a little earlier is pretty interesting. I think it's a common mistake that lots of people make when they look at the economy now. You said that 'they gave him good pay and benefits.' I think it's important to remember that employers don't usually give anything out of the goodness of their hearts in this country. Historically, it just hasn't worked that way. Manufacturing jobs were good jobs because of a series of historical events which put pressure on companies to make them good jobs. There's no intrinsic reason that running a cash register can't be a good job. How is it different than working on an assembly line except that you aren't being compensated and they are making tons of money off of you. These could be good jobs if the struggle was waged to make them so, but I don't see that happening."

Jerry: "Right, the union is too weak at Stop and Shop to do anything. They don't think of this as a real job where someone has to support themself. But, it's the only type of job available around here anymore. I'm never going to get out of the shelter at this rate."

The number of working people in Massachusetts who, like Jerry, are unable to afford housing increased dramatically during the 1990s. They cannot afford housing because of decisions being made on a corporate level. Many homeless people like Jerry worked part-time for minimum wage in places like the unionized Stop and Shop supermarket. The local store was one of 128 supermarkets that employed more than 48,000 people throughout New England in 1995. That year Stop and Shop reported $73 million in net income on sales of $3,789 million. The Chief Executive Officer received $1,198,153 in compensation (Spain and Talbott 1996: 1351). Yet, despite the profits and high executive salaries, many workers continued to be paid wages inadequate to afford housing.

Despite some popularly held beliefs about the laziness or learned dependence of "the homeless," many of the people I worked with were desperate to locate jobs and income. Most of the people using the shelter had some source of income. During 1995, 116 of the 193 people at the shelter received income from either paid employment or social security disability (SSI) payments. Over one-third of people staying at the shelter during 1994, 1995, and 1996 worked. However, most of these workers found themselves in low-paying food-service or agriculture jobs. Of the 69 employed people staying at the shelter during 1995, 42 worked in either food or retail trade for near minimum wage with no benefits.

Howard, an African-American male in his early 20s, came to the shelter when he could no longer afford to remain housed or attend the University of Massachusetts. Despite being an academic success throughout high school and his two-and-a-half years at the university, he had become homeless due to financial aid difficulties. Howard had been staying at the shelter for several months when he complained to me about how he had been working at Stop and Shop as a cashier for over 6 months and still could not afford to move out of the shelter. Despite a near perfect work record, he was still stuck with a part-time and inconsistent schedule paying minimum wage.

I asked if he had requested more hours. Howard replied that he was told, "you don't get to work full-time until you've been employed for a year." What was most frustrating to Howard was seeing the "Help Wanted" sign in the front of the store and seeing management hire people for more part-time jobs.

I then asked why he thinks Stop and Shop doesn't offer full-time hours. Howard replied, "cause they don't want to pay for benefits and they want to have you able to be at their call. Like yesterday. I wasn't scheduled, but they called me in to fill for someone else. They know you'll come because you're desperate for hours." The practice of not offering full-time work to employees until they worked in the store for at least one year was a management practice largely accepted by the local union. Many food service and retail trade employers follow similar practices, since this managed under-employment results in workers who are available to be called in at odd hours.

Adding to Howard's frustration was the inability of his United Food and Commercial Workers Union representative to understand his desperate need for more hours and greater pay. As Howard explained, "all they [the union stewards] do is tell me that we have a contract. That doesn't help me get money for a place to live." When I asked union leadership about the practice, they argued that they got the best contract possible considering competition from nearby non-union supermarkets. The "need" for large corporate profits and salaries for top management went unchallenged in the union's effort to work cooperatively with management.

The experiences of Jerry, Howard, and Jonathan are very much like the work experiences of many guests at the shelter. There are a number of possible ways of making sense of their work experiences. One could, for example, see these jobs as entry-level jobs that are "naturally" not very good jobs. The inability of these men to get a higher-paying job could be seen as the result of individual inadequacies and traits that must be reformed or retrained. Conversely, one could historicize these experiences within the larger socio-economic context of increasing inequality and the loss of higher-paying, unionized jobs over the past two decades.

In that sense, the work experiences of Howard, Jonathan, and Jerry reflect an overall economic shift in the region. In 1980, 20 per cent of workers in the county were employed in manufacturing. By 1990, this had dropped to 15 per cent. By 1991, 51.12 per cent of jobs were located in either wholesale and retail trade or services (Market Street Research 1994: 60). A 15-per-cent decrease in manufacturing jobs and a 12-per-cent increase in service-sector jobs occurred during the 1980s as manufacturing plants were replaced by restaurants, coffee shops, galleries, and large retail chains (Market Street Research 1994: 14). This trend continued during the 1990s. A 1999 study by the National

Priorities Project found that 61 per cent of the jobs with the most growth in Massachusetts paid less than what they defined as a living wage, with 42 per cent of jobs paying less than one-half of a living wage (National Priorities Project 1999). In addition, income inequality increased dramatically, with the poorest 60 per cent of Massachusetts residents experiencing a loss in real income since 1980 while the wealthiest 20 per cent of the state population saw incomes increase by 18 per cent (Bernstein et al. 2000). In Northampton, a 1999 study found 28 per cent of all families in the city making less money than they needed to make ends meet (Brown 2000).

The problem cannot, however, be reduced only to service jobs replacing manufacturing jobs. Instead, it is the type of service job available, the low pay in the available service-sector jobs, and the lack of any social movement or union organizing effort aimed at making these jobs into good jobs.

Most of the homeless people who find work are employed in food or retail trade, but not all. Many homeless people employed outside of food and retail trade continue to have a difficult time affording local rents. The wages paid in many jobs are simply not enough to pay prevailing rents. When the least expensive rent is close to $500 per month, it is difficult even for some "professional" workers to maintain housing.

Clearly, many of the people staying at this shelter were willing and able to work. They struggled daily to find employment in the city. Yet corporate practices resulted in the homeless person receiving wages inadequate to afford housing in the city. Often, these management decisions took place despite large profits. In fact, top management was rewarded with high pay and benefits for practices causing some workers to be homeless. Still, those practices remained virtually unchallenged.

A SEARCH FOR AFFORDABLE HOUSING

Like many communities, Northampton also suffers from a lack of affordable housing. A survey conducted in 1992 found that 15 per cent of Northampton residents mentioned the quality and cost of housing as a major problem confronting the city. In 1990, the median gross monthly rent for an apartment in Hampshire County was $526 per month (Market Street Research 1994: 53). In April 1996, I surveyed the cost of apartments listed for rent and found the average of listed apartments was $665. A 1996 study conducted by the University of Massachusetts Off Campus Housing Office found similar rents, with the average one-bedroom apartment costing $650 per month (Watson 1996: 16). The study also documented similar rents with low vacancy rates for neighboring towns. The National Low Income Housing Coalition found a mean rent of $706 per month for a one-bedroom apartment in 1996. They found that, as a result, 44 per cent of renters in Northampton were unable to afford market rate rents in 1999 (Dolbeare 1999).

What makes moving into an apartment more difficult is the practice of charging tenants first and last months' rent and a security deposit. This requires the average employed homeless person at the shelter to save well over two months' income. Clearly, such rents are out of the question for people with incomes ranging from $300 to $800 per month, as was typical of most shelter guests.

Given that the income available to most homeless people in Northampton is inadequate to pay "market rate" rents, the only affordable housing for most is to move into a rooming house or subsidized housing. Even these options are out of the range of many people. In May 1996, there were 259 single room occupancy (sro) units in the city, slightly more than one-half the number of units in the city 20 years earlier. The loss of sro housing in Northampton is reflective of an overall trend throughout the nation. "Urban renewal" efforts led to 18,000 sro units being lost between 1973 and 1984 in Chicago, more than half the sro units in Los Angeles being demolished between 1970 and 1985, and Boston losing 94 per cent of its rooming houses by the mid-1980s (Burt 1992: 34). These units once provided "affordable" housing for many people in poverty.

Even so, many of the people at the shelter do not even want to move into a rooming house. From their experiences and from hearing public representations, they find these places unsafe and inhumane. As one homeless woman, Ariel, put it, "you don't live in a rooming house, you survive, that's not a life." Unfortunately, though, even this type of housing is unavailable to many of the people at the shelter. When a 14-unit rooming house re-opened after renovations in February 1996, over 40 people applied to live in the building. Many of the 26 people who were not selected as tenants were still homeless in June of that year.

A second type of low-income housing once available was through government subsidies. Unfortunately, the waiting list for HUD Section 8 housing certificates or subsidized rooms and apartments in the city is virtually closed to anyone not categorized as "disabled" or elderly. Even these people often have to wait several years for a subsidy and then they need to locate an available apartment and a willing landlord.

For three days during September of 1996 the neighboring town of Amherst opened its Section 8 housing subsidy waiting list for applications. During the previous two years they had accepted no other applications. Workers at the shelter informed guests and helped them fill out applications, knowing that even qualified applicants would not come up for housing for several years.

One advocate, Elizabeth, explained this strategy in the following manner: "It's just something to do in case it ever comes through."

The local situation is a reflection of national trends. A 1995 report by the US Conference of Mayors reported that the average wait for Section 8 housing subsidies was 39 months. Applicants had to wait an average of 17 months from the time they applied until they received assistance (Waxman and Hinderliter 1995). As many housing authorities do not even take new applications, these numbers underestimate the demand for housing assistance. The National Coalition for the Homeless (1997) reported over 2.5 million people on waiting lists for Section 8 subsidies nationally in 1995.

One potential option for the homeless person is to look outside the city for a place to live. Rents in some surrounding communities are slightly lower and many of those who do qualify for housing assistance move out of Northampton. However, this is not practical for those trying to work their way out of homelessness through paid employment or who cannot afford a car. There is a low-cost (free during the academic year) bus service between Northampton and Amherst. In 1990, 62.5 per cent of the county's jobs were located in the three towns (Northampton, Amherst, and Hadley) along this corridor (Market Street Research 1994: 13). All but two of the employed people staying at the shelter during 1994 and 1995 worked in these three towns. As the following examples demonstrate, people finding themselves at the shelter go through a myriad of struggles to locate housing.

David, a white man in his early 20s, had been attending college until the previous year when he was hospitalized for depression. He was diagnosed as clinically depressed and thus had a low (approximately $430), but steady, monthly income from a social security disability check. David explained his housing search difficulties in the following manner: "At first, I was going to … take the first thing that came along, a rooming house or whatever. Then I said, that was part of my downfall. I can't just. In terms of my lifestyle, I can't live in a rooming house. I'll end up back in the hospital [for depression] if I do that."

Vin: "Just too many people with too many things going on?"

David: "I can't do it. I can't share a kitchen and a bathroom with forty people. It's hard enough here with twenty people. So, first I was going to find an apartment on my own and I can't afford that. Then, roommates in the paper, I started too late, I should have done it in August before all the students took up everything. So, now I'm waiting for someone to be able to pay for half an apartment. I had three or four people lined up and they keep backing out for money reasons."

Vin: "Could the staff do anything more to help?"

David: "Ultimately, I'd like to see one staff person who dealt with finding people affordable housing and getting them on waiting lists. Right now, even when Elizabeth [a social worker who was helping with housing searches] comes in, she gives you a form, she doesn't tell you what to do when you get down there. I went with Rob the other day to the Northampton Housing Authority and on the back of the form, Elizabeth neglected to tell us, I don't know if she's aware of this, before you go to the housing authority, you have to be turned down by ten places. Things like that. We just wasted our time."

Vin: "Have you tried Section 8 or getting on a waiting list for subsidized housing?"

David: "I'm on the waiting list for a lot of things. There are places in town. I see friends who have apartments that I can afford, but they fell into them through knowing people. I haven't been back in Northampton long enough. The people I know are the people I went to elementary school with. I haven't been back.... It's been ten years between living in Northampton. So, I lost all those contacts. I don't know the right people.

"I'm just crossing my fingers right now. Hoping that someone will have, be able to afford half an apartment. I'd be happy to move in with Rob, but he doesn't have any money. But ... Howard, at first I was going to do it with Howard, but Howard only makes like $70 a week. That's a problem if you're working in one of those jobs. He's making $5 an hour and he's not getting 40 hours a week, that's for sure."

Ultimately, David was able to find a roommate at the shelter and was one of the four people who moved from the shelter to an apartment in the city. He was luckier than most in many ways. His diagnosed disability provided him with a steady income. This diagnosis proved vital when he found an apartment because Elizabeth was also able to access money from the Department of Mental Health for the security deposit.

He is a quite friendly, intelligent, and engaging young man who got along with all those working and staying at the shelter. During his stay at the shelter, David's previously developed liberal political leanings became radicalized and he soon became deeply involved in the local Food Not Bombs chapter and spoke at several local meetings on homelessness. Several staff members welcomed such rare political activism and became eager to work with David to find him housing. The staff provided all the assistance and information they had available. Several guests were enthusiastic about moving in with David as a housemate. He frequently searched the local papers and approached real-estate agents for various housing options (such as renting a house or large apartment with several people), but none of these schemes worked.

David grew up in Northampton in a well-off family. Although his family hadn't lived in the city for several years, David maintained connections with friends from years ago who proved helpful as references and in searching for apartment rentals. When he found a potential apartment, his mother was willing and able to lend him the money necessary to move. Most of those staying at the shelter do not have close families, or their families do not have money to lend.

All of these exceptional factors had to come together for David to locate an apartment in the city after a several-month search. Most of those finding themselves at the shelter are not quite so lucky. Working with staff, budgeting and attempting to increase their incomes, applying to rooming houses, filling out forms to be placed on waiting lists, searching the newspapers and real-estate listings, and attending housing search workshops simply do not result in many homeless people being able to afford or locate housing in the area. The efforts of Susan and Jenny exemplify these struggles.

Susan, a woman in her late 50s, stayed at the shelter during the summer and autumn of 1996. She searched for a room or apartment on a daily basis for over three months. Susan, who became homeless in part as a consequence of events following her divorce from a long-term marriage, explored newspapers looking for places she might afford with her social security check, but with little luck. When she became frustrated with trying to find her own place, she called several people who placed ads for roommates. This didn't work out either. As she explained, "they are always kids. This town isn't a place for someone like me. There are a lot of places for people in their twenties just starting out. They don't want to live with me." The expectations about student age renters in this area results in decreased opportunities for older homeless people. Not giving up, though, she continued to search these options.

In addition to the standard techniques of finding a place to rent, Susan even began going door to door asking about possible apartments. Staff worked with her to place her name on waiting lists for every subsidized housing or low-cost housing option in the area. However, the prospects of Susan receiving help were rather dismal. Finally, she attended housing workshops at the shelter. Susan found all the suggestions and advice ineffectual as she still could not find affordable housing.

After months of unsuccessfully trying to locate housing, some staff became frustrated by the lack of people moving out of the shelter and the huge waiting list. Susan described the help she received during this period: "For every single place I looked at, they said take it. Take it. Take it. Take anything. And there was no basis for them to recommend it, except they wanted me to take any place. As long as I was out of the shelter, I was no longer their problem."

Leopoldina, Elizabeth, and Karen eventually decided that the solution to Susan's inability to locate housing was to give her a firm deadline for when she would have to leave the shelter regardless of whether she had a place to live. Susan replied, "I don't know what else I can do, but I'll keep trying. It's not that I want to live here under these rules. I just have no place to go."

Susan finally located a shared living situation with the help of staff. She moved into an apartment with two other women in a suburb of Springfield where the rents are much lower. Unfortunately, staff did not inform her that the women she had selected as roommates were long-time abusers of drugs and used alcohol as a coping mechanism. After three weeks in that apartment, Susan was desperate to move out. She called me at home to ask for help in having the staff at the shelter help her find a new place to live. "I really made a mistake, but I felt like I was being pushed out of the shelter. I have to find a new place. Do you think Karen or Leopoldina or Elizabeth will help?" Unfortunately for Susan, there was little the staff could do. There was no housing that she could afford. Once she moved out of the shelter, the staff just didn't have time to continue to help her look for housing that simply didn't exist.

In March, Susan called me at home at a few minutes before midnight to again ask for help. Her roommates were drunk and using drugs in the apartment. At that moment, a police officer was in the apartment arresting one of her roommates. Susan was in tears and desperate and had nowhere else to turn. I, however, couldn't really offer any real help either except to talk with her and reassure her that the difficulties were not her fault.

Eventually, Susan told me that what she was most upset about was that the shelter staff members hadn't informed her about the behaviors of her housemates. She said that the staff made her feel that she just had to move anywhere and that it was her fault she couldn't find an apartment. Her housing options were constrained by her limited income, no automobile, and the high rents in the area. As Susan told me, "they have all that staff at the shelter, but they don't do anything to get more housing in town. Plus, all those student volunteers come, but all they do is clean the shelter. That makes it a clean place to work for the staff, but it doesn't help us with housing."

A slightly different situation occurred with another group of shelter guests. When I describe the housing data to academic or policy audiences, a frequently asked question is, "Why don't three or four of the homeless people just share an apartment? College students don't have much money and they do it, why can't homeless people?" Unfortunately, it's not that simple.

As with David and the following example, many younger shelter guests do consider sharing an apartment with other shelter residents. Yet they often have a difficult time accumulating the security deposit and finding a willing landlord. Some landlords are willing to rent to groups of college students, but the lease signing is predicated on the students' parents co-signing the lease and agreeing to pay for damages. These options don't exist for most homeless people as neither they nor their relatives have the wealth or resources necessary to secure a lease in this manner.

An additional consideration is that of covert landlord discrimination. In Massachusetts, there is no specific law banning a landlord from discriminating against a tenant based on their being homeless. Many shelter guests tell stories of apartments being mysteriously taken shortly after they inform the landlord of their current address. It is likely that many landlords share the dominant cultural assumption that people become homeless because of something they did wrong. Because they lack a strong credit or reference history, many landlords decide not to rent to homeless people.

As an example, three homeless people became close during their stay at the shelter in 1994 and decided to attempt to locate an apartment together. The two women were working through a temporary agency at food-service jobs and the man received a monthly check from social security. Searching for a place they could move into on their incomes, though, proved futile.

One of the women, Jenny, explained, "The thing that really fucking stinks is that we've got enough money to pay rent and free up three beds. Then there'd be three people who really need them with beds here, but there are just no apartments. You need a million dollars to move into a place. They need more affordable housing. We shouldn't need to be here any longer. We've got jobs and enough money. I'd be willing to pay $525 or even $600 for a two-bedroom place, but this $650 or $700 is crazy. You need almost $2,000 to move in and even then there are just no openings. We've been calling all day. We asked one place if they'd have an opening by October 1st and she pulled out two drawers of waiting lists and said 'what do you think?' It's depressing. No wonder everyone thinks I'm going crazy." These three guests searched the nearby communities for an apartment they could share for three months. They had an advantage over most shelter guests in that one of them had a car and, therefore, they could live off the bus line. Yet they were unable to find an apartment to share in the region. Two years later, all three of these guests continued to struggle to maintain separate places to live.

These stories and data serve to outline the highly stressful economic and housing conditions that working homeless people struggle under every day. The wages paid (or incomes from government benefits) are inadequate to afford available rents. Homelessness is the result. However, this is only part of what needs to be analyzed in order to comprehend the social processes leading to homelessness. This information describes the material conditions of homelessness and describes how many homeless people do work very hard to resolve homelessness. However, little new insight is gained into understanding why homeless and housed people perceive and respond to homelessness in particular ways or why conditions of such socio-economic inequality are allowed to occur. To do that, one also needs to consider the discursive dimensions of homelessness.

Insight into the dynamics that have resulted in these strategies and predicaments can be gained through an analysis of both the material conditions in the city and how shelter staff and guests attempt to deal with this problem. It is important to contemplate both the economic conditions and how such conditions are discursively accepted or resisted. In this manner, it is possible to conceive of homelessness as the result of complex social processes that provide many potential avenues for resistance and political organizing. In that regard, the next section outlines policies, strategies, and negotiations undertaken by homeless people, shelter staff, policy makers, and local advocates in their efforts to address and resolve homelessness locally.

Responding to Homelessness: Reproducing the Deviancy Model

How are we to understand the conditions described above? I suggest that one way of understanding how a distribution of resources where many citizens live on the streets and in shelters continues is through examining the discursive conditions that coincide with these material conditions. An analysis of how people accept or work against homelessness is one possibility. Given the data about housing costs and employment, it is telling to contemplate the different strategies employed by shelter staff, homeless people, and community activists. Examining the practices by which people attempt to confront homelessness yields data on two fronts. On the one hand, a focus on practices helps us to understand the struggles undertaken. However, an analysis of discursive languages and practices also provides valuable insight into how the problem of homelessness is conceptualized and how some potential practices and policies are silenced. How do some strategies, policies, and practices become normal, routine, and common sense while others are understood as non options? What possible resistance efforts and public policies are silenced when some practices are considered natural or unchallengeable and others are deemed unrealistic and thus are not even considered?

What are some of these strategies? A wide range of responses are possible, but which approach is followed is constrained by how the social problems are conceptualized. One could, for example, look at some of these data as evidence of a lack of job skills or job readiness among the homeless. A thoughtful policy solution might then entail the implementation of practices aimed at developing the human capital of these potential workers through job training and educational programs. The assumption is that homeless people who agree to develop their own capacity to serve business as human capital will be able to get higher-paying jobs.

Another possible reading of these data is as evidence of the effects of deindustrialization in the United States. Policies might then be developed to offer incentives such as tax breaks that would lure manufacturing employers to the area in the belief that this will aid all citizens.

These are just two possible responses from a broad range of potential strategies that might be advocated by policy makers, shelter staff, and homeless people. Other potential efforts might strive to increase the supply of affordable housing, increase government benefits to those declared disabled, increase the number of housing subsidizes, alter tax plans, improve conditions in rooming houses, unionize service workers, increase the minimum wage, or even alter how surplus value is appropriated and distributed. The possibilities are endless. Yet, despite the clear data suggesting that the particular problem of homelessness is one generated by socio-economic processes and housing policies, the most commonly utilized strategies of responding to homelessness do not address those dynamics.

One alternative response sometimes employed by some homeless people is that demonstrated by Anthony. Anthony, a white man in his early 40s, stayed at the shelter on three different occasions during the five years of my research. Most frequently he traveled throughout the country trying to survive. He offered a rarely articulated perspective on the link between employment, wages, and homelessness. However, his strategy for dealing with homelessness was in many ways a quite popular one in that it remained an individualized strategy.

Anthony: "The whole situation here is a hopeless proposition because this is a very expensive town to live in. You have 25,000 college kids here with daddy's Visa card. I've seen time after time. The majority of people that are living here [at the shelter] are working fast food joints for almost minimum wage. First and last months' rent? Don't even bother with it. Much less, esoteric junk like cable and a telephone."

I then asked Anthony how he explained his own homelessness: "Is it that you don't feel like working for five dollar an hour jobs and not being able to make it because it's not enough to really live on so why bother?" My assumption was that Anthony had chosen not to work as a form of alter-hegemonic resistance against what we both understood as exploitative labor processes. Anthony is clearly a very bright and insightful man with no easily diagnosed disorders. To explain his homelessness, I assumed that he had "chosen" to be homeless and travel the country. That explanation made sense to my sensibilities, but Anthony offered a different perspective.

Anthony: "Well, that's what you think? (laughing) Ah, who am I to dispute you. No, I've worked at many jobs. I could show you a resume. I've worked at a casket factory. I've worked in the forest service, worked for landscapers many times, groundskeeper at a cemetery and at a private tennis complex in

Boston. I've been a truck helper delivering cabinets. I've cleaned out septic tanks. Last winter I was working part-time washing dishes for a friend of mine in Maryland.

"I certainly worked all my life. I worked, coming home from junior high school, feeding thirty head of beef cattle. I grew up working constantly on my parents' farm, but that was cool. My father worked at nights at the steel mill. I bought my own school clothes. I do have a work ethic. At times I rebel considering that I have three and a half years of college education and I can't get a decent job. I rebel against the fact that I've never made more than $5.50 an hour, except for when I fought fires for the fire service and you get paid time and a half.

"I think that if I really wanted to give in to society's strict rules, get a haircut and work at some factory, not a steel mill or a car plant where you can make real money, but just some factory someplace in New Hampshire. Of course, even those jobs are getting pushed out. But, then, I would not be homeless, but I am not willing to work at the old casket factory. I worked there for a couple months doing day labor, but I worked there every day and went early to make extra money.

"I don't want to work that job. I want to go back to school. I don't know. I don't owe any money on loans. I'd like to go back to school and pursue interests in conservation. I think my dream job would be eventually to go to a good school and get another degree. I've got two associates degrees, but maybe a four-year degree at a good school in horticulture."

Vin: "But, there's tons of money for drug treatment programs. If you said that you were pathological and needed someone to fix you, there'd be money."

Anthony: "How kind of you to bring that up. Here again, if you're an alcoholic or drug addict and you see that light, then all of a sudden cost is no problem. We're going to get you into a drug or alcohol rehab and maybe even a vocational rehab. It's the same old song. We're gonna take this person who's really trashed out and make them a valuable member of society, but the only problem I've got with alcohol (laughing) is that I really can't afford Korbel champagne."

Anthony continued, "I've never seen anyone in the situation that showed any interest in helping me go to school. It's not like I want to go to school and get a Masters degree in English literature. I want to go back and get.... In fact, this summer I was in Ohio and I tried to go to this school. They just flat out told me they were not interested. This might well be the best school for forestry, logging, and parks and recreation in the whole country. I went to them and they told me that they don't have any money for me. They are giving all their money to the welfare queens to go back to school and learn to be a nurses aide, not even a practical nurse. It's so they can get them off welfare and have them give up welfare and all the fringe benefits for making $5 an hour changing bed pans." [Although Anthony's words sound like a racialized complaint, other interactions throughout our relationship made it evident to me that, while disparaging of welfare recipients, Anthony is more critical of welfare reform efforts.]

"So, why do I think I'm homeless? I guess I have an easy cop out. In some situations, the wages are so low and the rents are so high that it's virtually impossible for me to not be homeless. I could take some absolutely terrible job, like I said before, let's say like in the old casket factory, but I really hate the thought of doing that for the rest of my life."

Anthony offers a very clear, thoughtful analysis of increased structural inequities in the United States. He is very explicit in articulating an understanding of socio-economic changes and in situating his personal struggles within those broader changes. He is willing to work hard when employed, but he feels that he then deserves decent pay. He longs for the days when a worker like his father could enter a unionized factory after high school and support a family. He feels powerless to alter these conditions, though, and tends to conceptualize only individual based strategies. As a result, he "chooses" simply to cope with being homeless and travels the country from shelter to shelter. He maintains the hope that somehow he'll manage to return to school and, with his enhanced credentials, might then be able to obtain a job paying enough to live.

It is important to consider what is marginalized in such practices. It is popularly considered unrealistic to try to fundamentally change the local distribution of wealth, wages paid at local businesses, or any of the fundamental or subsumed class processes. Decisions regarding the appropriation, production, and distribution of surplus value produced remain outside the scope of the dominant homelessness discourse. Prevailing dominant class inequality remains commonsensical. Likewise, it is understood that little can be done about the cost and availability of local housing. Even when non-dominant efforts raise the possibility of effecting change in these areas, they are marginalized by being deemed unrealistic and not worth pursuing.

When all attention is focused on reforming the individual, coping with exploitative conditions, feeling powerless, or trying to simply increase the number of shelter beds and subsidized housing, more systemic and structural factors often go unchallenged. The current social order and relations appear to be natural, inevitable, and common sense. Policies suggested to challenge this order often seem irrational and are understood as impractically "ideological." Practices aimed at altering systemic inequalities in the local setting do not take place. Decreasing capitalist exploitation or making the many service jobs in the community "good jobs" that pay living wages remains unrealistic. Current social relations appear to be natural and therefore unchallengeable. The efforts are then focused on how to cure, control, or manage the "disease" of homelessness, not at all construed as a problem with any racial, gendered, or class dimensions. The logic behind most prevailing discursive practices seems to be that, if the homeless person were fixed or reformed in some way, there would be a job available paying a wage adequate for that person to be housed. This does not, however, appear to be the case in Northampton. Many well-trained, hard-working housed and homeless people are working for low wages in food-service jobs. Yet the thought that we could work to create a society where everyone is meaningfully employed in non-exploitative labor and housed seems unrealistic. Homelessness persists in part because the structural and discursive conditions causing it remain largely uncontested in daily practices.

In Northampton it appears that prevailing economic practices are not considered a variable to be contemplated in developing strategies to confront homelessness. Instead, it is taken as a given that decisions about production, appropriation, and distribution of the local surplus will remain in the hands of a few. Resistance to the discursive and systemic dimensions of homelessness will not be organized. Consequently, it is accepted that food-service employers will pay low wages, offer no benefits, and offer most workers only part-time hours. These conditions will be tolerated because of the prevailing assumption that there is nothing that can be done to alter them. This sense of powerlessness results, in part, from both hegemonic assumptions about the perceived naturalness of capitalist economic relations and the belief that capitalism is too powerful a system to effectively challenge.

CHAPTER 2

Medicalizing Homelessness

ANTHONY: *"They always come across with the same rap. It's the same stupid rap that the alcohol and drug abuse programs use. 'Give us this person for one month and you won't believe what you'll see. They'll be driving a van and move in next to you and start buying that suburban house, 2.3 kids.' It's all shit. I've traveled around this country for several years now and I've never seen one of those programs that really does what it says."*

GLORIA *(a staff member and volunteer):* *"I think many staff take the sort of disease model approach still. Well, you know if that's your problem, we'll hook you up with meetings, you'll do this, you'll go into this program, and that will cure your problem and fix you."*

On a June night in 1996, Maria came downstairs and asked if she could speak with me. The conversation began with Maria, a woman with a long history of activism against racism and exploitation in the community, attributing her staying out the night before to a growing state of depression that she was now willing to admit. Maria had been in the shelter for several months by this time and had, consequently, learned to approach staff by indicating cooperation with designated self-help treatment plans.

Maria said, "I'm going to try to get a counselor on Monday. I'm starting to feel really low. It started at the end of the week and by Friday and Saturday, I didn't want to see anyone. My friend called me yesterday and I went over there to help her. I thought it would make me feel better to help someone else and get out of here for a little while. It worked for a little while, but about 6:00 I started feeling sad again and ended up crying. I went to help her out and here I was crying and she had to comfort me."

I asked, "Why are you feeling so depressed?"

Maria: "I feel stuck here. I need a job. I've done everything I can think of to get a job. I even applied at Burger King for an assistant manager, but the manager was some young kid who said I was too qualified. I've sent out my résumé to a thousand places, but I can't get a job. I'm starting to think that I must be doing something during the interviews to turn these people off. I know sometimes it's discrimination because I'm someone who speaks my mind and sometimes they don't like Puerto Rican women who speak up, but

I'm starting to blame myself also. Thinking that there is something I'm doing wrong."

Vin: "Well, I don't know what to say. What you need is a job that you feel good about so that you can get some money and get out of here. Maybe you should see a counselor, but only if it's to have someone to talk to so you don't blame yourself. Often, though, all people here get from counselors is more self-blame and medication. But, sinking lower and lower and feeling worse about yourself because you can't get a job won't help you either."

Maria: "I know. When I came here I thought I'd get a job right away, but I've been here for almost two months now and I still don't have a job and now I'm starting to feel like it's my fault. [Maria had worked with several staff members and friends to retool her résumé and sent out copies to every social service or social justice agency in the region during her first week in the shelter. Every staff member thought that she'd find a job and move out quickly.] I think I'll call this woman I used to talk to a few years ago on Monday because she was pretty good. Except she tried to push the pills on me. I need a job. A job don't come in no pill. If you got a pill that gets me a job, I'll take it, but I haven't seen any pill like that yet."

Maria then went on to explain how she had been to several interviews. At three different jobs, her lack of transportation was a serious obstacle. So, at the latest interview, she lied and said she had a car. She said that she'd just save the first couple of checks and get one somehow. She said, "I'm not stupid. I know why I'm here. Just because I'm homeless doesn't mean I don't see what's happening in the society at large and in my own family, but what can I do?" Unfortunately, what Maria, usually a strong, nurturing, energetic person who had a long history of employment in the social services, was trained to do through the routine case management "help" at the shelter was to learn to blame herself and treat her individualized self.

Maria is just one of many homeless people who come to blame themselves for being homeless. They come to ask, "what is wrong with me that I am homeless?" rather than "what societal conditions have changed to allow for widespread homelessness in the US?" Consequently, rather than working in collaboration with other people struggling against structural violence, she responded to homelessness by trying to detect, diagnose, and treat perceived problems within herself. This chapter explores how the well-meaning, routine helping practices within shelters help produce such practices. As I outlined previously, many homeless people and advocates believe that they are powerless to alter conditions of inequality in any significant manner and they therefore focus attention on individualized coping strategies. This is part of the answer to the questions I posed in the introduction, but other dynamics also need to be considered to understand the durability of homelessness.

In the next three chapters, I explore how popular individualized discourses interact with neoliberal conceptualizations within the homeless sheltering industry to produce understandings and practices based upon a medicalized hypothesis of deviancy. A bio-medicalized conceptual environment where responding to homelessness through practices aimed at treating disorders within homeless people has become the framework within which homeless people, policy makers, shelter staff, and advocates operate.

While many cities have opted to criminalize homelessness, federal agencies and other communities have responded by advocating a "continuum of care" approach. Under this model, communities develop programs to treat symptoms thought to create homelessness and shelters offer the services understood as necessary to help people obtain housing. As a result, a wide range of social service programs function to help homeless people treat their disorders and "transition" out of homelessness. These practices are part of a broader effort undertaken by some advocates and policy makers to reframe homelessness away from a problem of bad individual choices and toward a model whereby homeless people would be portrayed as the victims of disease and dysfunction. The goal is a more effective and caring response to homelessness, but, as Merrill Singer and colleagues have argued, the move toward a disease model often has ambiguous and conflicting impacts (1992).

Recent efforts have increased services to reform and retrain individualized homeless people. These efforts do improve the lives of some individuals who are homeless. However, the continuum of care approach does not fundamentally address questions of access to, and distribution of, resources in the community. In fact, I found the focus on "disease" within the discourses of "helping" actually obliterated discussions of alternative explanations. Undoubtedly, this outcome is in part the result of a combination of both dominant imaginings and stigmatized perceptions about homeless people and the impact that funding concerns have on influencing public priorities and sheltering industry practices (Lyon-Callo 1998).

One effect of conceptualizing social problems through a lens of diseased bodies is often a neglect of systemic inequality. Consideration of the material and historical conditions that might contribute to the production of problems is silenced or marginalized by a focus on individual traits and habits. As Vicente Navarro describes, the medicalization of social problems plays the ideological function of legitimizing existing class relations and serves to "depoliticize what is intrinsically a political problem. Thus, within a medical framework, what requires a collective answer is presented as an individual problem, demanding an individual response" (1986: 40). Navarro argues that much of what is thought of as illness is in fact the result of a fundamentally disproportionate distribution of resources.

Similar dynamics apply to homelessness. Arline Mathieu, in her study of the medicalization of homelessness in New York City during the 1980s, discusses how representations of "the homeless" as mentally ill by government officials served to marginalize the political-economic context of homeless people (1993). She details how press releases by the mayor's office in support of a policy of randomly taking homeless people off the streets by force emphasized that the people still living on the streets were homeless due to mental illness. Mathieu argues that as long as homeless people were bio-medically represented as deviant, their living on the streets could be "solved" by housing them in shelters and forcing them into treatment programs. Attention to systemic inequities that contribute to producing widespread homelessness was thus deemed unnecessary.

Through my work, I have come to agree that systemic inequities contribute to the production of many behaviors that are commonly read as pathological disorders among people without permanent shelter. Reading these behaviors as individual disorders certainly plays a role in silencing work against exploitative social conditions and in limiting our ability to work more effectively against the conditions that the work documents. However, there is another component that deserves analytical attention. Something much more subtle and insidious than simply mystification takes place when homelessness is medicalized. Routine, everyday practices undertaken by shelter staff and guests to resolve "diseases" actually reproduce and reinforce dominant imaginings about homelessness and homeless people and thus contribute to produce particular subjectivities, experiences, self-images, and behaviors among homeless people.

To make this argument, I draw upon insights coming out of the critical-interpretive approach in medical anthropology represented by Alan Young (1995), Robert Desjarlais (1997), and Margaret Lock and Nancy Scheper-Hughes (1990) as well as by scholars outside of anthropology writing on the production of medicalized knowledge, governmentality, and the practices of self-making. These scholars demonstrate how all knowledge of society, normality, illness, and self is socially produced and determined and that all knowledge about the body, health, and illness is constituted through historically situated cultural negotiations (Lock and Scheper-Hughes 1990). To analyze that process it is imperative to examine the techniques and practices through which people who are without a permanent place of residence are made into subjects to be governed by their selves, social workers, social planners, and medical experts. In this book, therefore, I outline a strategy for considering the ways in which the homeless body (the social body and the body politic regarding homelessness as well as individualized homeless bodies) is, in part, produced and reproduced by social practices within homeless shelters.

Many of the people who volunteered, worked, or lived at this shelter articulated understandings supporting the view of homelessness as embodied deviance prior to even being connected with the facility. This is hardly surprising given the preponderance of public discourses that pathologize poor people. Yet, in analyzing precise practices in the shelter setting, I uncover how the well-intentioned efforts within the shelter actually work to reproduce and reinforce this image of homelessness as a social problem with an origin in individual deviancy. Reformative efforts often focus on "treatments" that fit within constructed views of normal and deviant. These practices produce subjects who come to understand reform of the individualized self as the most "reasonable" and "realistic" ways of resolving homelessness. Through their experiences in the shelters, many homeless people are thus produced (and reproduced) as political subjects who are more likely to engage in self-blame and self-governing than in collective work against structural violence.

Additionally, with the medicalization of social problems, it becomes common sense to understand the coping strategies of homeless people as symptoms and evidence of mental illness. Through such a medicalized understanding, homeless people are understood as passive victims of biological disorders rather than situated agents: "The medical gaze is, then, a controlling gaze, through which active (although furtive) forms of protest are transformed into passive acts of 'breakdown'" (Lock and Scheper-Hughes 1990: 68).

In a similar vein, Alan Young argues that what we need in analyzing biomedical practices is not simply to unmask or demistify truth from ideology, but rather,

> a critical understanding of how medical facts are predetermined by the processes through which they are conventionally produced in clinics and research settings. Thus, the task at hand is not simply to demistify knowledge, but to critically examine the social conditions of knowledge production. (1982: 277)

To understand the social conditions of knowledge production in regard to homelessness, I analyze precise practices in the shelter setting. In such an analysis it is also important to be aware that the effects of a bio-medical discourse both produce popular conceptions of "the homeless" and help to construct normalcy. Reformative efforts are thus often focused on "treatment" efforts to homogenize the population to fit within constructed views of normal and deviant. The professed aim of medicalization is to heal or normalize the homeless person so that they can house themselves, yet I will show that medicalization also has the effect of determining who is deserving and undeserving of housing.

If we are to understand the durability of homelessness despite the well-meaning efforts of a nation-wide sheltering industry, we must contemplate how "the homeless" and "homelessness" as categories are produced and resisted. These categories are products of discursive conditions that give rise to concrete ways of thinking and acting. We need to examine practices designed to validate these categories. Similarly important, though, is the need to consider how these conditions create routine practices that normatively silence or devalue other possible ways of perceiving and being in regard to homelessness. Whereas Mathieu (1993) and Hopper (1988) primarily focus their studies on how the medicalization of homelessness affects city government responses, I analyze how the dominance of this bio-medical model serves to constrain resistance practices by both homeless people and their advocates.

Medicalization within the local setting

In comparison to other shelters, the Grove Street Inn is considered an exemplary facility by both staff and guests. The staff I worked with prided themselves on providing substantive help to homeless people. Guests at the shelter almost uniformly convey their appreciation for the more humane atmosphere offered them there while describing it as one of the safest and most helpful shelters that they encountered. As one guest put it, "despite all of my complaints about how I'm treated here, I still think this is the best shelter in all Massachusetts. For the most part, staff here actually care about us and treat us like humans."

Anthony, described the shelter in slightly different terms. He told me that he was surprised that "you actually have some staff who seem to be human beings." He then continued, "I have the ultimate respect for anyone who wants to change this society for the better. If anyone has humanistic urges, it's a very stressful job. Unfortunately, I don't see a lot of people who are working with homeless people who have that as their motive."

My analysis is slightly different from that articulated by Anthony. Whereas Anthony sees the primary problem as being one of punitive motive and mistaken intentions, I see them as well-meaning people working within the parameters of a medicalized discourse. Many of the staff do voice a profound desire to change the society for the better, but their actual practices focus on detecting and reforming homeless pathologies. Under the rubric of doing good work and providing substantive help, staff and homeless people participate in institutional activities designed to reform and normalize "the homeless." Agents within the industry develop diagnostic tools, statistical representations, and reforms to treat homeless people by making them into a new kind of person. Under these conditions, the staff and guests function to govern "the homeless" through a regime of surveillance, discipline, and personal enhancement. In short, a "normal" person is to be made through governing "deviant" homeless people. This chapter begins to detail the governance of homelessness, accomplished according to routine shelter practices aimed at detecting, diagnosing, and treating disorders of the self within homeless people.

Techniques of Diagnosis: Detecting Deviancy

Efforts to detect and diagnose individual causes of homelessness began shortly after a person arrived for an available bed. The new shelter guest was quickly directed into the staff office for an intake interview. The intake serves several main functions. It is an opportunity for the staff to compile some statistical data about the person, to start a "case history" that is used to guide case management practices throughout the person's stay at the shelter, and to outline rules and procedures for the new guest. Of paramount importance, though, is the fact that the intake interview is the first opportunity for the staff and guest to diagnose what disorder(s) of the self caused that person to be homeless or, as staff say, "what issues" that person has to work on.

One of the first steps in developing a case history on each homeless person is to have the guest and staff look for the factors that have had an impact on that person. A defining feature of the diagnosis is that the homeless guest must be a willing collaborator. Guests are taught to ask, "How did I come to be this way?" It is this reflexive inquiry that is at the heart of the reform efforts operating within the shelter.

Staff and guests gather this information in a variety of ways. One specific question on the intake form, for example, asks the person to state their "reason for homelessness." There are a number of suggested reasons: substance abuse, mental illness, domestic violence, eviction, loss of income, being new to the area, or being chronically homeless. As most homeless people already have been taught to exhibit a great deal of self-blame, many guests respond by disclosing a self-reported behavioral or training problem within their self.

In addition to the required components of this intake, the staff member works to comfort the recently homeless person who is often quite nervous about being in a shelter. A caring staff member uses this as an opportunity to develop a sense of rapport with the new guest and explains how the staff might be able to help with housing. An added benefit of this more informal discussion is that, from the homeless person's mannerisms and articulations, the staff member begins to gather observational data used to diagnose possible pathologies. If, for example, the staff member "detects" possible mental illness or substance abuse, they will note these observations in the person's folder and in the staff log. Other staff members can thus be aware of this diagnosis and look for supporting (or contrasting) evidence in their future interactions. The staff and guest's determination of cause "types" the homeless person as a kind of client defined by signs of his or her disorder. This typing drives subsequent treatment responses.

Once guests and staff learn that the cause of homelessness lies within their selves, their efforts "naturally" focus on diagnosing that deviance, not on structural inequality. If, however, the staff member interacts with the new guest as a fellow person struggling to make sense of and survive within the world and less as a professional who is there to reform the homeless person, a different type of relationship is sometimes possible. I have taken part in rather lengthy discussions with homeless people about systemic causes of homelessness and the problematic nature of stereotyped visions of homeless people guiding social policy during the intake. These conversations will then often continue throughout the guest's stay at the shelter. These guests are often more willing to contemplate and discuss possible resistance against systemic contributions to homelessness and their critiques of shelter practices.

While most staff relish these political discussions, they are seen as peripheral to the real work to be accomplished. While acknowledging that systemic factors play a role in homelessness, staff still need to detect what within that individual are the particular causes of homelessness. As one staff member, Karen, put it, "really, I do see the bigger picture, but we have to do what we can to really help the people coming here. The actual work is dealing with the individual person."

Formal efforts to diagnose possible causes of homelessness continue throughout each guest's stay. A case management meeting is scheduled for the newly arrived homeless person to meet with day staff for a second intake during the first week in the shelter. While the initial intake form is ostensibly just an opportunity to gather basic information about the guest, explain the rules, and get the homeless person acquainted with the shelter setting, the second intake is more clearly defined as establishing a counseling relationship. At this meeting, the staff and guest meet in the staff office to discuss what "issues" brought the person to the shelter and what resources are available in the area. A more detailed case management intake form asks particular questions about level of education, employment history, medical history, past therapy or counseling experiences, and any background with substance abuse or mental health treatment programs.

This information is used to determine what problems the guest should work while at the shelter. Detected symptoms range from severe mental illness to a need for employment re-training due to decreased manufacturing employment in the region, but all "causes" are discursively understood as problems within the homeless person. Within a week of entering the shelter, the homeless person becomes a case history to be treated through case management of perceived deviance.

An additional formal diagnostic practice occurs in weekly staff case management team meetings. At these meetings, staff discuss the behaviors and actions of each person currently staying at the shelter. Any observations or interactions that other staff members might have recorded in the staff logs are used as data for uncovering disorders and developing treatment plans. Most of the meeting is spent diagnosing what disorder is causing each person's homelessness. As one staff member, Leopoldina, described, "what we do is sit around for an hour and bitch about what is wrong with each person staying here." Again, any insights garnered from these meetings are supposed to be recorded in the guest's case history so that all staff can better help the homeless person focus on understanding and treating their disorder.

With the initial diagnosis in hand, the shelter staff and homeless person proceed to look for evidence to support, refute, or alter the diagnosis over the next few weeks. Surveillance and monitoring of shelter guests is a second method whereby staff and guests work to diagnose and reform disorders within homeless people.

SURVEILLANCE AS A DIAGNOSTIC TOOL

Surveillance takes place in monitoring the guest's obedience and fulfillment to shelter rules, while counseling guests, playing cards, resolving conflicts, overseeing the cooking of meals, and engaging in informal discussions. A focus on monitoring guests is stressed in the design of job descriptions for any new staff positions. Ann, an ex-staff member, commented, "whenever you are at the shelter you are supposed to be monitoring the house and the guests." These practices seem like common sense to many staff and guests.

While monitoring guests for "symptoms" of disorders routinely takes place during informal interactions, the everyday surveillance of homeless guests is most explicitly enacted under the rubric of enforcing shelter policies. The surveillance is understood both by many guests and by staff as an additional mechanism for detecting deviancy and, thus, "helping" to reform homeless people. When a homeless person enters the shelter, she or he is confronted with an overview of shelter rules and procedures. During the initial intake meeting in the staff office, the staff member details three pages of shelter policies and procedures and obtains the guest's agreement to abide by these regulating mechanisms. Most shelter policies are designed to operationalize staff and guest monitoring and disciplining of guest behavior as means of detecting what caused their homelessness, creating the opportunity to treat those pathologies through regulating and disciplining the bodies of homeless people.

Rules are enforced to regulate when homeless people can be in the shelter and when they must leave. Policies regulate smoking, eating, what rooms they can go into, and when they must be quiet. Those who are staying in the shelter must receive staff permission to stay out past 8:00 pm and may not return to the shelter after using drugs or alcohol. Other rules regulate how guests must treat each other and interact with staff members. Still other policies mandate that those staying at the shelter allow staff to check rooms on a daily basis, that guests must check in with staff when arriving and leaving, that staff are to check guests for the use drugs or alcohol, and that guests must allow staff to search personal belongings.

When staff monitoring (or guest disclosure) reveals a rule being broken, a written warning describing the transgression is signed by both staff and guest and placed in the guest's case folder. A conversation often follows where the staff member uses the violation of shelter policies as evidence of an issue that the homeless person needs to "fix" to have any hope of becoming housed. In some cases, immediate referrals to outside expertise will follow as the homeless person is hospitalized for mental illness or sent to a detoxification program. These practices are portrayed as a mechanism by which homeless people can be made to come to grips with the issues (always disorders within their selves) causing their unstable lives and homelessness. Two shelter policies exemplifying this logic are those on "disrespectful behavior" and "substance use."

One shelter rule states that "no disrespectful behavior is allowed." This very general rule, in practice, serves many functions. One is to ban any public or private affection between guests at the shelter. Guests are given warnings for having sex in bedrooms, cuddling on a couch, or even holding hands in the living rooms—all evidence of "disrespectful behavior." When I asked other staff members why cuddling and sex were banned in the shelter, several staff argued that many of the men and women in the shelter were "survivors" of childhood assault and suffered from post-traumatic stress disorder. The assumption is that they are neither able to make "good" decisions about sexual partners nor emotionally able to witness other guests hugging or cuddling without triggering a traumatic episode. Therefore, the response is for staff to help these deviant selves through banning any public affection between guests (even those who are married or in long-term relationships). Furthermore, whenever a shelter guest does display affection toward another person, this is most often diagnosed as a sign of their "acting out" due to past traumatic abuse.

I'm not suggesting that some (and perhaps even many) homeless people have not experienced physical and sexual abuse in their past. Such abuse is all too real in the contemporary United States. However, when staff and homeless people come to believe that such abuse is "the cause" of their homelessness, this guides practices by which they address homelessness. Surveillance is thus made necessary. These practices produce "the homeless" as deviant in that all affection is viewed only through the lens of a psychiatric disorder. Monitoring guests' affection and sexual practices thus becomes a mechanism for potentially "helping" them resolve their homelessness through receiving therapeutic treatment for childhood abuse.

A second example is the rule banning any homeless person from returning to the building after using drugs or alcohol. Many people have been given warnings and tossed out of the shelter for violating this rule. Staff are trained to smell the breath of every guest arriving at the shelter and to search for other signs of substance use. The articulated logic behind this policy is the deep-seated belief that substance abuse is a factor causing the homelessness of many shelter residents. According to this logic, a person who is "using" is not ready to be housed or sheltered. If the staff want to help, they need to detect substance use and confront guests about their drinking in order to break down "denial."

Housed people drink and may even abuse substances daily, but in the shelter all use of alcohol and drugs is classified as evidence of abuse. One absurd example of the logic of this rule occurred in 1993. One guest, James, had been staying at the shelter for close to two months. He went to work each evening canvassing for an environmental organization and spent his days writing an historical novel. Throughout the ongoing surveillance by staff, alcohol was never detected on his breath.

One Sunday evening James came back to the shelter and excitedly came into the office to tell me about his afternoon. He had been sitting in the bar of a local restaurant watching soccer during the afternoon hours that the shelter was closed when someone he knew happened to come into the restaurant. His old friend bought him a beer and they spent the afternoon reminiscing. When he told me this story, I listened and shared his excitement, but then replied that, unfortunately, that meant that I had to give him a warning. He was understandably shocked, as his behavior appeared completely sober.

When, with James's urging, I brought up at a staff meeting how ludicrous I felt giving James a required warning, two staff members responded that he was in "denial" about his substance abuse and post-traumatic stress disorder (PTSD). When I explained this to James, he replied, "That's nice. I go to work every day and never cause any problems. Because I'm homeless though, I'm an alcoholic if I have a beer with a friend." The warning stood and Donna, the assistant director at the time, spoke with James in a case management meeting about the need for him to confront his alcoholism if he wanted to resolve his homelessness.

Unlike James, most homeless people I've encountered readily comply with staff diagnosis of symptoms of alcoholism, depression, a lack of job training, or similar disorders of the self. After enough time in the shelters, one enters into the discursive regime of disorders and begins to think of oneself as home-less precisely because of shortcomings within one's own individualized body.

As discussed earlier, enforcing the rules is not the only type of monitoring and disciplining of the bodies of homeless people followed by staff in their effort to diagnose and treat pathology within homeless people. In the search for detecting and diagnosing symptoms, seemingly innocuous behaviors such as watching television during the day, drinking alcohol, sleeping late, listening to loud music, or not washing one's dishes are transformed into symptoms of a diseased self. Watching television during the day, for example, has been por-trayed as evidence of depression, self-medication for mental illnesses ranging from schizophrenia to post-traumatic stress disorder, and evidence of a lack of self-esteem and self-responsibility.

If the staff want to "help" those staying there, they must be constantly on the look-out for any signs of aberrant or deviant behavior in all interactions. They are supposed to document and convey any of this evidence to other staff through the case file, staff meetings, and the daily staff log. Shelter staff and homeless people are trained to look for "causes" of homelessness in the personalized behaviors of individual homeless people. In this manner, the staff member's monitoring, diagnosis, and documentation in the case files are seen to index an internal state within the homeless person that has "caused" that person's home-lessness. Behaviors become "signs" of disorders that require treatment.

As Leopoldina reminded me after reading an early draft of this chapter, the range of disorders diagnosed at the shelter through case management meet-ings, intake interviews, and surveillance practices is much more prodigious than only those described above. Several "causes" in addition to the typically detected lack of work skills, depression, lack of self-responsibility, mental illness, or substance abuse are diagnosed. Some guests who drink alcohol or use drugs are portrayed as "self-medicating" to "treat" the effects of mental disorders such as PTSD or depression. They are then placed into the category of being "dually diagnosed" (having both mental illness and a substance abuse problem). Other homeless people are understood as "delusional," "bi-polar," "dissociative," or "learning disabled" based on observations of their guest's interactions with people. Increasingly, "borderline personality disorder" is used to describe any homeless person who does not easily fit into any of the other diagnostic categories. Two additional diagnostic terms are used to explain any homeless person who displays anger or resentment about the situ-ation they are placed in. "Passive aggressive" and "dry-drunking" are terms used by staff and social workers to transform the anger of some homeless peo-ple into a mental disorder. The well-meaning effort to work more effectively in helping homeless people coupled with the dominance of the bio-medical model of individual pathology drives these practices.

One example of the "dry-drunking" diagnosis involved Larry, a guest at the shelter in 1996. This 50-year-old, white former machine operator became homeless after he could no longer pay his rent at a rooming house from the odd jobs he was putting together. For close to two months while at the shelter he was in constant pain from an infected tooth for which he was unable to afford treatment. Despite also having an injured foot, Larry still managed to continue working at a variety of jobs and applied for a wide assortment of training programs during his shelter stay. He had not touched alcohol in the 14 years since his marriage ended, but steadily attended Alcoholics Anonymous meetings. Yet, when he sometimes angrily confronted guests and staff about the noise in the shelter preventing him from being able to sleep, some staff members transformed his anger at the situation into a diagnosed mental disorder. He was "dry-drunking," a 12-step term for an alcoholic who displays "drunk behavior" without drinking. Larry is just one example among hundreds of similar examples. There appears to be a diagnosable disorder for every homeless person.

Through the formal mechanisms of intake interviews and case management meetings combined with the less formal surveillance of homeless people, "symptoms" are detected. Staff and guests then use a variety of mechanisms and techniques for diagnosing a disorder and developing a treatment plan form the detected symptoms. While a few more formally trained shelter staff use the diagnostic tools provided in the DSM-IV, most guests and staff supplement the scientific, medicalized knowledge with less scientific diagnostic devices. Combining insights from 12-step, self-help programs with culture-of-poverty discursive understandings, they diagnose homelessness as being caused by a learned lack of self-responsibility, poor work ethics, "denial" about substance abuse, a lack of life skills, or mental illness. Through these practices, homeless people find the "cause" of their condition within their own self.

Treating Disorders: Producing Self-Governing Subjects

KAREN *(a staff member)*: *"I can't do my job if there are people here using drugs and unwilling to work with me. I don't see why we don't have drug testing here. Most other shelters do. Aren't we supposed to be helping them so they can help themselves? If someone's using drugs, they're not working on their issues. We're just enabling them."*

Once the staff and guests have detected and diagnosed one or more disorders, they then set to work on "fixing" those problems. Depending upon the "diagnosis," the treatment might take one of several forms. Homeless people are often referred to substance-abuse treatment programs, placed in half-way houses for drug treatment, sent to self-help counselors, medicated for mental illness, urged to seek job training, trained in improved life skills, or referred to mental health professionals in order to "resolve" their homelessness.

When analyzing the effects of treatment techniques, it is important to realize that not all "reasons for homelessness" are understood by shelter staff or homeless people to have the same type of cause. Some disorders (such as schizophrenia, attention deficit disorder, alcoholism, border-line mental retardation, or depression) are understood as being the result of bio-chemical dysfunctions within the body. Detected behavioral causes of homelessness (such as a lack of self-discipline, poor work ethic, or other so-called "dysfunctional" life skills), however, are often understood as having been caused by "cultural" or family dynamics. Other reasons for homelessness (including an inability to be paid a living wage, under-education, a need for retraining, or needed employment training) are understood as resulting either from "cultural" dynamics or sometimes from structural inequality. Yet, regardless of the cause of the disorder, the prescribed treatment is quite similar. Guests and staff work to reform and retrain the individualized homeless person's self.

Two interrelated forms of treatment occur within the shelter. Some disorders of the self are seen to require professional, expert help. When a homeless person is seen to need such expert help, a referral is often made outside of the shelter. This may take the form of therapy, job coaching, detoxification, or skills training. These treatments focus on administering to perceived disorders of the self. Many of those staying at the shelter, for example, are diagnosed with depressed or attention deficit disorder (ADD). In recent years, I and other staff have witnessed an increased reliance upon medication for guests referred to therapists and psychiatrists. Homeless people (like many other people in the US) are being medicated as a method of treating their "mental illness." Any contributions that social inequality and related systemic conditions play in the process of depression, for example, are transformed most often into bio-chemical disorders of the mind and of the individualized self. Why feel anguish or depression when one can be sedated with one of the many new psychotropic medications? Why examine systemic contributors to depression when one can simply homogenize brain functioning and, through the process of sedation, marginalize discontent as a mental illness?

Most routine treatment practices, however, do not involve a referral to outside experts. Instead, the staff and guest work together to develop case management plans designed to allow homeless people to help themselves. Throughout a homeless person's stay, he or she meets periodically with different staff members. The guest and staff review together how well the guest is resolving the problem of homelessness. If, for example, the guest is attempting to treat a diagnosed substance abuse problem, they will discuss how many 12-step meetings have been attended, acknowledge if there has been any recent substance abuse, disclose if a "sponsor" (a person who acts as a guide in a 12-step program) has been found, and discuss "sober" housing options. If a guest has been diagnosed as homeless because of a lack of job readiness, they might discuss how many job training programs the guest has attended, contemplate adult education or literacy classes, address how to fill out a job application or interact with an employer, or discuss attendance at résumé-writing workshops.

The case management plan differs for each person depending upon the level of compliance with the prescribed treatment plan. If a guest is not "working on their issues," the staff member might encourage them with images of a housed future or threaten them with the risk of being told to leave the shelter. Nevertheless, virtually all efforts focus on the homeless person being encouraged to understand homelessness as the result of something within the self that requires reform.

As a result, most responses to homelessness undertaken by guests at the shelter fall under the rubric of self-help and self-governing. The work of Barbara Cruikshank on self-help, self-empowerment (1994) and self-esteem (1996) programs for female welfare recipients is quite informative in laying out an analysis of the growing dynamic of self-help. Cruikshank argues that there has been a recent shift away from the technologies and interventions by which the poor have been governed since the middle of the nineteenth century and toward a new form of governing. This new form emphasizes that communities and poor people must learn to govern themselves by healing and treating their bodies from within, and without interventions by governing social authorities. Cruikshank describes these recent efforts as "promises to deliver a technology of subjectivity that will solve social problems like homelessness and inequality by waging a social revolution, not against capitalism, racism, and gender inequality, but against the order of the self and the way we govern our selves" (1996: 231).

Cruikshank argues that these practices often assume a natural subjectivity that is being repressed for one reason or another. There is an assumption that the self (the individual bodied self) is natural. Those advocating self-help do not pay attention to the extent to which personal life is governed and is itself a terrain of government, or the extent to which the self is shaped and constituted by power. The self, Cruikshank points out (like poverty, racism, and homelessness), is not personal but is rather the product of power relations, the outcome of strategies and technologies (1996: 248). Self-help, self-fulfillment, and self-esteem programs are technologies that produce certain kinds of selves and marginalize the possibilities of producing alternative kinds of subjectivities. Cruikshank suggests that people are made into subjects by external powers operating upon the self and by how people come to understand their self. Models of self-help and self-esteem programs teach people to look within their bodies for the cause of their difficulties. To understand the production of subjectivities, we must examine "what I say to myself ... what I do to myself ... how we rule ourselves" (1996: 248).

The same techniques happen routinely in the homeless sheltering industry. When case histories diagnose disorders within homeless selves and thus reinforce "knowledge" about deviance within people that "causes" homelessness, it is only "common sense" that efforts at treating these perceived disorders through self-discipline and self-government are prescribed and encouraged. Homeless people learn to ask themselves, "What have I done wrong?" and to look within themselves for possible disorders to treat and reform. Homeless people become self-governing subjects.

SELF-GOVERNING PRACTICES

Practices aimed at treating and reforming the self at the shelter take many different forms. Attempted remedies focus on "empowering" homeless people to take greater control over their (individual) lives through job training, improved "life skills," enhanced self-esteem through participation in shelter workshops, or participation in 12-step groups. Additionally, some shelter staff have suggested rules such as enforced wake-up calls, curfews for smoking cigarettes or watching television, and limiting hours when guests can talk or play cards. These suggested rules are conveyed as techniques for helping homeless people discipline themselves into becoming "normal" self-governing selves. Both guests and staff presume that such a path is the way in which they are then more likely to become housed.

The treatment for such disorders is accomplished through enforcing shelter rules as a mechanism for training homeless people in life skills and self-responsibility. A conversation with a shelter guest who was attempting to convince me that unmade beds at the shelter were an indication of the lack of self-discipline that was causing the homelessness of most other shelter guests typifies this belief. He argued, "You staff are too liberal. If you really want to help these people, you'll teach them some discipline." This is a common sentiment at the shelter. Curiously, he made his bed every morning and, yet, he was still homeless.

The enforcement of shelter rules trains homeless people in two ways. On the surface, there is overt disciplining. Staff members monitor guests as they do their nightly chores, maintain a log of who is in the house, check guests' rooms, check the belongings when a homeless person enters the shelter, and maintain a constant presence in the house watching for signs of drug or alcohol use. If it is discovered that a rule has been broken, a series of warnings possibly leading to expulsion ensues. An often-stated view, by both guests and staff, is that such scrutiny is the only way to teach some guests the discipline they need to help themselves.

The guest's agreement to abide by the rules during the intake procedure becomes conceptually important at this point. Emotionally, the signature on the intake form helps some staff members kick people out of the shelter. The view is articulated that "they choose to come here and understand the rules. If they don't want to abide by the rules, they don't have to stay here. We can't help them, if they won't work with us." This logic both helps justify maintaining existing practices and functions to silence critics. When I pointed out that a homeless person doesn't exactly have a wide range of choices to choose from in deciding to stay at the shelter, a frequent staff response was that "we can't let the inmates run the prison." The argument was made that staff would only be harming people at the shelter if staff were inconsistent in enforcing the rules, because that is not how the "real world" functions.

A similar logic justifies why homeless people are made to leave the shelter after receiving a second warning for drug or alcohol use. The warning and other documents in the client's case history are used as evidence that the person's homelessness is caused by substance abuse. By continuing to use the substance, the homeless person is neglecting the treatment for his or her disorder. It is understood, therefore, that by suggesting that the behavior might not be a sign of an addictive disorder, a staff member or fellow guest is "enabling" that person to remain "in denial." Within this logic, of course it makes sense to kick people out of the shelter in order not to "enable" them. These guests can return to the shelter only when they agree to become a compliant, self-governing homeless person treating disorders within their self. The staff use the technique of overt punishment to make the person "work on their issue." Often, going through a treatment program and pledging to attend a daily 12-step meeting is the only way that person is allowed to return.

I witnessed several additional efforts to manage, train, and empower "the homeless" implemented or suggested over the years. Based upon "culture of poverty" discourses, there is a widely held belief that many of the difficulties confronting poor or homeless people are complicated by their learned behaviors. Frequent reference is made to parenting techniques, the argument being that staff members need to think of their work as similar to training a child. It is important to understand that the suggested rules are all conveyed as techniques of treating what "caused" their homelessness by helping homeless people regulate their behaviors and become "normal" and presumably, therefore, more likely to become housed. The goal is to train the homeless person through a very structured set of strictly enforced rules so that they engage in self-reform. However, as with many types of governance and control, shelter rules work well only if both those enforcing them and those living under them believe that they serve a valuable function. Much like in policing, those enforcing the rules need to feel committed to them and those who the rules are enforced upon need to agree that they are beneficial. Once this agreement occurs, everyone involved is more likely to commit the energy and attention needed to enforce these regulating mechanisms. Yet nobody working at this shelter liked feeling that their job was to monitor and police homeless people or to give warnings. We wouldn't knowingly hire anyone who did, but being willing to engage in surveillance was seen by most staff as a necessary part of helping those who are staying at the shelter treat "their issues." As Hannah, a shelter administrator, described, "we're not doing anyone any favors by being too liberal and letting people get away with things."

Not wanting to come across as strict disciplinarians, though, staff endeavor to conduct such surveillance in a "respectful" manner. One staff member, Aaron, described this in the following way, "I was told during my training to just treat the people staying here like fellow human beings, but then I was also told that I need to constantly be monitoring them and enforcing the policies. I'm not sure yet how to do both." The accepted ideal for responding to Aaron's dilemma is for the staff member to create a strong presence, conveying that they are in control and knowledgeable about what is occurring without being confrontational or obvious. When they catch someone breaking a rule, staff members are expected to stress both how the rules are designed to help and how this transgression is further data supporting the previously diagnosed "cause" of homelessness.

Staff members find that, if they present an image of being willing to enforce the rules in a consistently strict manner, most guests will not try to challenge or break the rules. Similarly, just as many people welcome community policing and the increased search-and-seizure rights of police throughout the United States, those staying at the shelter often appreciate the efforts of staff to enforce the rules and regulations. In fact, most guests articulate a desire for more stringent enforcement of policies.

Anthony described his feelings about rule-breakers: "Toss them if they don't do their part."

Vin: "Do you think that if we were stricter it would help solve homelessness more or that it just makes it a more comfortable place to stay?"

Anthony: "Well, I think that these people obviously need more structure. Not the two guys [Tom and Jonathan] who work. They are very self motivated. But, a lot of these people. I think they are graduates of mental hospitals, graduates of jails, of alcohol and drug use programs."

Enforcing rules through the use of overt discipline is one form of government. As Michel Foucault describes in *Discipline and Punish: The Birth of the Prison* (1979), the enforcement of rules and orders often goes smoothly if people understand themselves as constantly under surveillance. In the case of an assumed panoptical vision, people will often discipline themselves to follow rules. Also, if people believe that other members of their community are a danger, they are often more likely to submit to increased control on their personal liberties. Both of these forms of surveillance occur on a routine basis at the shelter.

What works even more effectively to control homeless subjects, though, is when guests believe that these mechanisms of training and reform are for their own benefit. This is precisely where the more insidious forms of self-government come into play. Through the shelter practices and discourses of self-help, many homeless people internalize the view that they are in need of reform and that homelessness is a result of problems within themselves. The answer to their homelessness then takes the form of agreeing to retrain and discipline themselves.

The ideal at the shelter is an atmosphere with such a high level of self-governing and self-discipline by those staying there that the presence of the staff as an overt reminder of rules and procedures is unnecessary. Overt rule is one form of government, but, as Foucault makes clear, power is not just something that happens to people from above. Self-governing is also an apparatus of control. The role of self-government draws attention to a dimension of our experience constituted by all those ways of reflecting and acting that shape, guide, manage or regulate the conduct of persons—not only other persons but also oneself through self-governing.

This is the second function of the shelter rules. In addition to being a form of detection, they are also seen as a technique of training. Homeless people are taught that they are in need of self-help and it is in their best interest to self-govern. But let me say clearly that I am not suggesting that self-governing homeless people come about through the clearly intentioned efforts of staff members. Rather, the social milieu of self-help and medicalization within which both staff and guests function internally suggests that these practices are the most helpful ways of responding to homelessness.

Although total self-governing has not been achieved at the shelter, it is very rare for a shelter guest to openly question a rule. Instead of trying to change rules or case management practices, those who disagree often learn to comply. As Susan, the homeless woman discussed previously, stated, "they [the shelter staff] treated everyone badly, but you have to accept things. I had things written about me and was treated badly for things I never did. Real intrusions into my life. But, there's nothing you can do about it. I have nowhere else to go and they think they're helping."

If a homeless person does voice an opinion against routine shelter treatment practices, thus indicating their non-compliance with rules or case management efforts, their resistance against shelter norms is often understood by guests and staff alike as a very symptom of their homelessness. The experiences of Raymond, an African-American guest with a long history of social activism and community organizing, exemplify this practice.

Raymond was one of the few guests to openly question shelter policies. He would spend much time arguing against staff efforts to diagnose his behavior as the reason for his homelessness and against what he saw as inhumane shelter policies. He would inform anyone willing (or sometimes not willing) to listen that homelessness was the result of poverty and racism. Raymond urged staff and guests to acknowledge that they should spend time changing the behavior of corporate and governmental leaders if they wanted to solve homelessness, not try to alter behaviors of poor people. He told me, "Sometimes I just can't believe how stupid people staying here are. They know they're being oppressed, but won't say anything about it."

After admitting that I also sometimes have similar thoughts, I offered Raymond an alternative explanation. I suggested that often homeless people find the cause of their homelessness by interacting with the sheltering industry, popular culture, and "common sense" understandings. They blame themselves for the condition of being homeless precisely because of the kinds of knowledge about homelessness that are currently prevalent. The deviance hypothesis of explaining homelessness as the result of disorders within homeless people has become the dominant part of the conceptual space in which they live. The hegemony of this model has made it difficult (but not impossible, as Raymond and Anthony exemplify) to think and act any differently.

Raymond agreed, but then offered a further contributing explanation: "Right. But also, if you do speak up you will suffer for it. I've always spoken up when I see injustice and I've been labeled a troublemaker and am banned from many places. But you have to speak up or you're just as bad as the oppressors. You're cooperating with them."

I agreed with Raymond that staff do punish guests who don't cooperate. Staff were contemplating making Raymond leave the shelter because he was uncooperative with case management procedures. But, I also suggested that the combinations of self-blame, prior encounters with social service institutions that do not welcome or respond positively to client-suggested improvements, the depth of awareness of self-help ideas, and the threat of being denied a place to sleep for not "complying" with the prescribed treatment plan might have a very real effect in silencing many homeless people.

Raymond is not the only homeless person who has had the experience of being punished for speaking up against shelter practices or for not cooperating with the deviance model operating at the shelter. If a guest openly questions shelter policies, staff (and often other guests) regard them as a problem. Almost always, the homeless person is diagnosed as misplacing their attention on "political" matters. Expressing concern about inequality or critiquing shelter rules is often portrayed as evidence of mental illness, characterized by the symptoms of "dissociative behavior" and "paranoia." If a guest disagrees with the staff member, the staff member describes resultant interactions in that person's case file and in the staff log. Medication has even been suggested in these recorded notes and during staff meetings as a means of "helping" non-compliant guests who speak out against what they see as unjust shelter policies and practices. Non-compliant behavior is thus turned into a medical problem.

Although Raymond portrayed the choices available to shelter guests as a dichotomy between clearly intended, public, oppositional acts and cooperating with oppression, other people staying at the shelter do not comply with treatment efforts in different ways. As evidenced by the number of written warnings given by staff for transgressions against shelter rules, some people demonstrate their disagreement with policies and treatment efforts through subverting or breaking shelter policies. However, I have never witnessed these behaviors being described by either staff or guests as resistance against shelter practices. I suggest that such an understanding is unlikely precisely because most people at the shelter do not have the conceptual framework to do so. The bio-medicalized environment produces the understanding that these non-compliant behaviors are evidence of passive manifestations of disorders within particular homeless people, not acts of invested social agents.

Most people staying at the shelter, though, readily learn to comply. They willingly ask for more structure while engaging in a significant amount of self-governing. Either they have come to understand their homelessness as the result of personalized dysfunctions or they have learned that to retain housing they must comply. These self-blaming opinions are often used by staff to justify existing shelter procedures and to marginalize critiques. It is hardly surprising that this occurs, given how routine "helping" practices teach homeless people that they are in need of such normalizing reform. The staff often feel that such techniques are the only tools they have to help their clients.

On the surface, the shelter policies and procedures serve the rather benign purposes of assisting homeless people with self-responsibility and ensuring safety in the house. On a more subtle level these policies are mechanisms of power and self-governance. Many homeless people internalize the view that they are in need of reform and that homelessness is a result of disorders within their individual body. By reinforcing these taken-for-granted assumptions, shelter staff and guests play a partial role in constructing such dominant discursive conditions and are complicit in the silencing of alternative resistance efforts. The attention and focus on individual deviancy reinforces and produces feelings of self-blame and the need for self-help, as the following examples indicate.

THE COOPERATIVE GUEST

One hot August night in 1993 I had a long conversation with Jenny. She was struggling emotionally with her inability to find housing. Jenny, a 29-year-old woman, had come to the shelter almost three months previously with a friend of hers. They had moved from the Midwest in the hope of finding a less oppressive community for lesbians in Northampton. Within a few days of entering the shelter, Jenny had found a job washing dishes at a local restaurant. As she put it, "I've always worked and have no trouble finding work. It's finding work that pays enough to live on that's hard."

Jenny had started employed work in her early teens. The best paying jobs she had were in manufacturing businesses, but those jobs were increasingly difficult to locate both in the Midwest and the Northeast. Fordist production plants had been largely eliminated by the mid-1990s as new technology, the drive for increased productivity, and management decisions aimed at consolidating surplus value in the hands of a few resulted in fewer higher-paying industrial jobs. As a result, Jenny (like millions of other workers) found herself working for low wages in service work.

As Jenny and her partner stayed in the shelter, the staff began to work with them on detecting and treating the issues thought to have made them homeless. As Jenny unsuccessfully searched for a better job, case management meetings switched from a focus on finding employment and housing in a new city to what was wrong within Jenny that was preventing her from obtaining a "good" job.

Increasingly, these case management meetings focused on Jenny's life history and asked her to be reflective about her personal relationships and behaviors. A view was voiced at the staff meeting that Jenny was suffering from PTSD and co-dependency and that these mental disorders made her spend too much time focusing on other people. Jenny's habit of worrying about and caring for other guests was portrayed as an unconscious effort to divert her attention away from a focus on her own problems. Several staff attempted to counsel Jenny through pointing out her "disorders" and offered "reality checks" where they made clear how she was unhealthy. Behaviors (such as Jenny offering advice or counsel to another homeless person) which various staff members had identified as symptomatic of her disorder would be brought to her attention. Often, both Jenny and the staff member would link these behaviors to past family dynamics. The diagnosis was that Jenny was simply repeating a harmful cycle of caring for others instead of working on her own mental health and emotional stability.

Jenny said, "Everyone's been telling me that I'm nuts so I must be. One of the staff told me the other day that I should go see a therapist. She said that I drove Abby [her friend with whom she had moved to the area] crazy through my co-dependency and telling her what to do. Is it being crazy to worry about people you care for and want to push them to become their very best?"

She told me that she went to see a doctor because she'd been having neck and back pain. Jenny reported that the doctor told her that it was just a tight muscle and was probably due to stress. The doctor prescribed Valium as the cure for her back pain. Her response to this encounter was, "I must really be crazy. I have a sponsor [a person who plays almost a mentoring role in Alcoholics Anonymous] who's co-dependent and says that I am. Donna tells me to go to a therapist, and now this doctor gives me Valium. I don't even know who I am any more. I've got some ego thinking that everyone can't survive without me, but I've always managed to survive myself. It's also hard hearing from people my age who have done so much with their lives. I can't even think of what I'd like to do. If I do and fail, then it's worse than not trying."

Jenny was not alone in her experience of being "helped" at the shelter. I have taken part in many similar conversations and witnessed similar treatment practices time after time at the shelter. Jenny was under a great deal of stress. She was homeless, her time at the shelter was running out, she could only find low paying work, she couldn't find a place to live, and the registration on Abby's car was about to expire. Yet the only response to her homelessness was through attempts at treating the diagnosed mental illness within her self. She tried therapy, medication, 12-step programs, and employment counseling. None of these efforts, however, altered the regional wage scale or employment opportunities. Three years later, Jenny was housed but still struggling in poverty as she worked at low-waged jobs and attended self-help meetings.

After a few months of trying to move out of the shelter, Jenny, like Maria and dozens of other homeless people I worked with, was learning to conform to the belief that the solution to homelessness came through treating the self. Case management practices encouraged them to believe they were powerless to alter any socio-economic or systemic conditions. While contemplating being medicated for mental health problems, Maria stated, "a job don't come in no pill," but neither Maria nor Jenny had access to any way of responding to their inability to resolve their homelessness that did not involve self-pathologizing. Rather than providing an alternative way of understanding their situation, routine practices within the shelter produced feelings of self-blame.

Let me repeat that my concern is not with whether or not substance abuse, depression, schizophrenia, or post-traumatic stress is real. Certainly, some homeless people do use what I might consider excessive amounts of drugs and alcohol, and these activities do often contribute to problems for some people. Similarly, many people who come to the shelter are quite distraught, perhaps depressed, over the situation they find themselves in. Other people like Jenny do display characteristics that are commonly viewed as signs of "mental illness." Of course, many people who come to the shelter have had traumatic episodes in their lives. I'm not disputing that these are "real."

My concern is that these very "real" understandings produce the range of permissible activities for both staff and guests. Through dominant discourses of medicalization and self-governing, people are taught to understand homelessness as the result of disorders within individual selves. Homeless people are rewarded with extended stays and increased staff "help" for cooperating with these practices. This leads to concrete practices by which concerned people respond to homelessness and marginalize other possible understandings.

The practices outlined in this chapter both produce homeless subjectivities and contribute to reinforcing a dominant conceptual image of "the homeless" as deviant individuals. These practices are technologies that produce homeless subjects. It is hardly surprising, therefore, that widespread social movements challenging social inequality do not take root in the sheltering industry. Homelessness becomes medicalized as both staff and homeless people discursively learn to resolve this social problem through diagnosing and treating disorders of the individual bodied self. Case management produces compliant homeless selves intent on "normalizing" their (individualized) selves through self-governing behaviors and assumes a contrasting "normal" self. The idealized self is a particular kind of person reinforcing the common understanding of homelessness as an individual problem of the self and not a result of, for example, cultural or political-economic processes. Once constructed, categories such as "mentally ill," "victim of the foster care system," "substance abuser," and "veteran" become essentialized as the determinants of homelessness.

These subjectivities lead to certain questions remaining unasked and certain policy proposals being deemed "unrealistic" or even unimaginable. In focusing attention on retraining, reforming, empowering, and caring for the homeless subject, the exploitative social processes that create homelessness go unchallenged by many of the homeless themselves, as well as by their advocates. In this manner, discursive practices create homeless subjects. But something else is also occurring with taken-for-granted shelter practices. Hegemonic understandings about "the homeless" as particular types of people are also being produced.

CHAPTER 3

Shelter Statistics and the Silencing of Systemic Concerns

ANTHONY: *"I think, they grossly misrepresent the homeless people as fitting those categories because the more they can push the idea that the majority of the homeless are drug addicts, mentally ill, or alcoholics, the more that they can guarantee that, if you give us more money, we'll provide the services, we'll fix these people up, so to speak. Once again, 'they'll be back to the suburbs. After two months with us, Jim is going to head off to the burbs just like you. 2.3 kids, split level house.' This is not going to happen. What are they really going to say? Are they really going to say that it's the American system where the wages are too low and the cost of living is too high? Are they going to run around and just simply say that the capitalist system is simply wrong? I don't think so."*

In addition to routine case management and surveillance, additional everyday shelter practices contribute to reproducing dominant conceptions of "the homeless." One such practice is statistical record keeping. As post-structuralist studies have shown, statistics are embedded with power and subject effects (Hacking 1986, 1991; Urla 1993; Rabinow 1989). Statistics help create understandings about "types" of people by measuring attributes of particular categories of peoples and putting people into populations to be managed, governed, and normalized (Hacking 1991). Because they are popularly perceived as objective representations of social phenomena, statistics are often given widespread credence as non-subjective and empirical data. Examining both what statistical data are maintained at the shelter and how they are utilized yields further insight into how routine shelter practices serve to produce "the homeless," reinforce social policy based on managing these presumed others, and marginalize alternative resistance possibilities by reconfirming "common sense."

As the social science of statistics developed, collecting information about the poor became linked with the project of social reform. It grew into a technology for diagnosing and mapping characteristics of populations. Modern statistics became a technology of individuation as statistics began to function for the determination of differences between people (Rose 1991). Statistical representations thus were critical elements in emerging technologies of the social aimed at "helping" the poor, for example, by reforming and retraining individual members of these aberrant population groups. Examining statistical record keeping practices at the shelter indicates much the same happening.

How then should we do an analysis of shelter statistics? There are several possible ways of examining practices of statistical record keeping within the shelter. One possibility is to focus on the reliability and accuracy of compiled data. Statistics and written records are compiled regarding a wide variety of characteristics and life experiences of homeless people. Some politically useful outcomes could come from an analysis of the accuracy or reliability of shelter statistics which might overestimate the number of homeless people with histories of substance abuse or mental illness. However, my focus is on analyzing how specific statistical compilation practices have come to make sense and how they function to produce typologies of homeless subjects.

My concern is not simply with the accuracy of statistics or the fact that the chosen categories of analysis mask social facts. Rather, all statistical representations are social constructs coming out of, and contributing to, particular sets of social knowledge and social relations. It is an analysis of the uses of this mechanism, coming out of a particular social and historical understanding (the deviance model), as a means of social analysis producing homeless subjects and "the homeless" in which I am most interested.

To do that analysis, I examine and problematize a range of record-keeping practices. What precise statistics are maintained at the shelter, what is their origin, and how are they used by staff, guests, and policy makers? Conversely, what statistics are not kept and how does that lead to the marginalization of possible understandings and practices? What kinds of categories are used in official reports to governmental agencies, what specific categories of information are maintained on official forms, and what kinds of classificatory schemas inform the record keeping? How do both formal and informal record keeping practices generate statistical categories of specific "types" of homeless people and how do these get linked to specific symptoms of disorders and put in motion certain kinds of treatments?

The need for that type of study became quite clear to several shelter staff members at the Grove Street Inn when they saw how homeless people were represented in a 1995 grant application to the Department of Housing and Urban Development (HUD). Hannah, the shelter grant writer and administrator, claimed in this grant that 82 per cent of people staying at the shelter the previous year were technically disabled due to mental illness or substance abuse. The grant application caused a large uproar in the shelter when two staff members, Ann and Gloria, read and distributed it. They were quite upset and argued that the numbers were completely inaccurate.

When Ann and Gloria asked Hannah about the accuracy of the data she said that she simply used the statistics that Donna, the shelter director, had given her. Donna just compiled the numbers from the initial intake forms and the compilation of data from guest case histories. "From these, you get the 'fact' that 51 per cent of the people here supposedly have had, at one point or another, substance-abuse issues, 14 per cent had both mental health and substance abuse and, whatever the remaining percent is have mental health issues. That's where the numbers came from and, therefore, they are all disabled." This grant application used data compiled at the shelter to argue for more funding for case management positions. These positions would ostensibly assist homeless people through providing counseling services for their mental-health and substance-abuse issues. Based on our routine record-keeping practices, the statistics were "accurate," yet they were still quite troubling. This demonstrated to me the need for analyzing origins of the categories and forms that the numbers were based upon and how these statistics were then being used to justify shelter policies and practices.

Beginning with the initial intake interview, the staff record and compile a wide assortment of data regarding people at the shelter. Staff maintain demographic information such as age, self-defined race, sex, and home town of guests at the shelter using the initial intake form. Additional information regarding where people go when leaving the shelter, reasons for homelessness from the intake form, case-management diagnosed causes of homelessness recorded from case management practices and informal staff observations of the homeless person's behavior, and staff treatment referrals (how many people are sent to day treatment programs, job training programs, etc.) is compiled.

These statistical representations about "the homeless" and about how the program operates were compiled on a monthly, quarterly, and yearly basis. The statistical reports were used in a number of ways. Monthly reports were sent to the Massachusetts Department of Transitional Assistance, the Northampton city planning department, the shelter advisory board, and other funders of the program. Both the city government and HUD received six-month reports to help monitor the number and "type" of people at the shelter, and how well the shelter did in helping homeless people.

Shelter administrators also use statistical information to construct an image of the "typical shelter guest." In this manner, statistical profiles are used to determine "causes" of homelessness. These profiles of "typical guests" then help in developing programs, determining staffing needs, and defining the role of staff. Staff and shelter administrators use the data as guides to assist with case management and as a means of determining unmet needs. Shelter staff seek to find information about those staying at the shelter to work more effectively in resolving the issues contributing to the person becoming homeless. Funders and policy makers need data on "the homeless" so that they can develop policies and programs for managing this social problem on the local, state, and national level. This all appears as fairly benign, routine, and non-controversial.

Traditionally, the motivation for recording and compiling statistical representations at the shelter was multi-faceted. Shelter staff, including myself, simply collected the data that made sense to them and what information was requested by funders, grant applications, and shelter administrators when this research began. The information that made sense to collect, though, was limited to data on town of origin, race, age, sex, veteran status, last address, "documented" mental-health and substance-abuse issues, referrals to treatment, referrals to training programs, "reasons for homelessness," and where people go when they leave the shelter.

A related reason for the compilation of statistics was ostensibly to increase knowledge about the social problem so that appropriate social policy might be developed. The city planning department, for example, was provided with a quarterly statistical profile of who used the shelter and where they moved to when leaving. They used this data, for example, when Donna and I informally agreed that we believed that we were serving more and more younger guests and we searched the intake files to document an almost two-fold increase in guests between the ages of 18 and 26 from 1992 to 1994. Donna then examined the specific case history files in an attempt to ascertain characteristics of the homeless teens. The hope was that, once we uncovered why they were becoming homeless, we could then develop effective programs to help them. Looking at the files, she came up with a few "profiles" of "typical" homeless teens. One "type" was the responsible and hard-working cooperative guest who was lacking education or job skills. The second "type" of guest discovered was the more "difficult" guest who didn't follow shelter rules, was uncooperative around the house, and was not employed. Once these typologies were documented, grants were written to fund a treatment plan developed for each "type." The planned treatment for the "responsible" young homeless person included job training, résumé-writing skills, and mentoring from potential employers in more skilled labor. For the "difficult type," the treatment plan included more closely monitored structure with a clear set of rewards and punishments desired to teach them needed self-responsibility. The statistical typologies compiled from shelter records set in motion a series of efforts supported by the local planning department.

Most statistical data provided to funders, local officials, and on grant applications were simply pulled from what staff routinely compiled during intakes and case management. What is important to recognize is that none of us considered these recording practices as important or controversial at first. Later on, when I asked, most staff said that they were too busy doing the important work of "helping" homeless people to concern themselves with thinking critically about statistical record keeping. Yet, for some of us, the power of statistics to reinforce or possibly undermine dominant conceptions about, and within, homeless subjects became clear after the HUD grant application debate. The following portion of the staff discussion demonstrates some of the new awareness of the power of statistics brought on by that application.

Donna (the shelter director): "Rachel, Hannah, and Allison [the shelter administrators who wrote the application] are fully cognizant of the fact that disability doesn't cause homelessness. They agree with you and the thing was that the guidelines of the proposal were so narrow in terms of it being just money for people with disabilities. It was basically a way to speak to HUD in HUD's way."

Ann: "They can make it vague like it is. But, they still are going to get two case managers, five intake workers, and three outreach workers to do case management, intakes, and outreach. It's not going to be to do education, organizing, or community development."

Donna: "Who is saying those positions can't do that. You are. They're not. No, seriously I just want to look at that."

Gloria: "There's nothing about organizing in there. Part of it, I think, is that no matter how vague it is, the direction that's being proposed just reproduces the belief that there is something wrong with the people staying here that needs to be fixed. What else can you get out of a grant saying that only 18 per cent of the people who come to the shelter are homeless because of wages or insufficient jobs or cost of housing."

When Gloria, Ann, and I began to look more closely at the recorded data it became clear that our statistical record-keeping practices were not so inconsequential after all. The information was being collected and used to develop a typological profile of "the homeless" through the compilation of demographic and statistical data. These data reinforce prototypical understandings about homeless people being homeless because of deviance within their selves. As such, it becomes easy for political leaders and shelter professionals to simply replicate essentialized categorizing of homeless people.

Funding requests for statistical profiles on "the homeless" come from various government entities and granting agencies. Funding applications most often necessitate demonstrating through empirical data how successful your program has been at fixing and reforming "the homeless" through job training, self-help, or counseling so they can "transition" out of homelessness. As Hannah described it, "they want to see that they are getting the right bang for their buck."

The shelter received significant state funding for the first time in 1995 through the state Department of Transitional Assistance (DTA). The DTA required the compilation of statistics in a monthly summary of how many males and females used the shelter, how many people were served meals, and how many were referred to mental-health, job-training, and substance-abuse services. To Hannah and other administrators, the form was completely inconsequential and non-controversial. We depended upon the DTA for funding and this reinforced the need for "continuum of care"-driven case management and record keeping.

Some staff, however, were very upset when they received copies of the DTA form. As Leopoldina said, "The choices of referrals are so limited. Nowhere do they ask how many exploitative businesses you picketed this month. Their concern is in how many ways we are working to fix individuals. If we buy into their game, we'll be limiting ourselves even further." Of course, though, the shelter staff continued to send the form to the DTA. What else could we do?

The taken-for-granted, everyday practices of shelter staff are based upon and, in turn, reinforce a particular problematization of homelessness. If practices within the shelter were not based upon a perception of "the homeless" as pathological and deviant individuals, different questions might be asked that would lead to the compilation of different statistical data used in a variety of ways. All of the information compiled at the Grove Street Inn at the beginning of this study focused on "the homeless" without contextualizing any of it within the larger political-economic setting.

In analyzing statistical record keeping within the shelter, it is also important to consider one other thing. The power of a hegemonic understanding, such as the bio-medical discourse operating within the shelter, does not come just from making some ways of being appear normal or natural. The medicalized understanding guiding these practices serves to marginalize and silence non-dominant possible ways of acting. In that light, it is important to consider what possible statistical representations did not take place and how they were marginalized by the focus on treating individual homeless people.

As one example, until 1995, the Grove Street Inn never compiled information regarding the number of people being denied a bed. The underlying assumption guiding this was clearly that the role of the shelter was to diagnose and treat those homeless people within the walls of the shelter building. Only when the shelter could not meet the increasing demand for shelter beds without people sleeping on the floor, did we begin to document this need. Documenting the unmet demand for shelter beds necessitated the creation of a new record-keeping device, the waiting list, which I compiled. Hannah and Donna then utilized these compiled statistics about the increased overall unmet demand for shelter beds to lobby city planners, local clergy, and local funding agencies. However, their focus remained on the need for more shelter beds and more treatment programs to train and treat homeless people. Data showing homelessness as resulting from increasing poverty and inequality during an historical period of great prosperity for some were not used.

Staff could have provided a wide range of alternative views of homelessness through available statistical information. They could have collected data on the increasing frequency with which shelter guests were prescribed anti-depressant medications or denied medical care coverage. Such data could be used as an entry point for developing an understanding of effects of the growth of managed care within the mental-health industry on both public health and homelessness.

Statistics compiled at the shelter could be used to document the gendered construction of mental health and substance abuse as "causes" of homelessness. For example, 50 per cent of females staying at the shelter during 1996 were categorized as mentally ill, while 18 per cent were diagnosed as abusing drugs and alcohol. The data for males was 27 per cent with a perceived mental illness and 56 per cent as substance abusers. Similarly, demographic data on the racial composition of guests show the disproportionate representation of those self-defining as Black, Hispanic, and Native American. During the first nine months of 1996, for example, the shelter served people in the following self-defined racial categories: 12 per cent Black, 16 per cent Hispanic, 2 per cent Native American, and 70 per cent White. This is compared to 1.6 per cent Black, 2.6 per cent Hispanic, less than 1 per cent Native American, and 92.6 per cent White in the county. These data could be compiled along with information from the 1990 US Census to document evidence of structural racism in Northampton: for example, the per capita income of Black residents was less than one-half that of white city residents, and poverty rates for Hispanic residents were twice that of White residents (Massachusetts Institute for Social and Economic Research 1990).

Similarly, data could have been compiled documenting how over 35 per cent of the women who came to the shelter were leaving violent domestic situations. Linking domestic violence and economic dependency for many women to homelessness could inform a range of social policies and resistance efforts. Arguments could be framed for the need for more battered women's shelters, more efforts to prevent domestic violence, or for developing strategies to ensure adequate income and housing for all women. Equally significantly, looking at homelessness in these terms creates a setting for the homeless person to understand their homelessness as a shared, collective experience.

Such data could be used to broaden the scope of local policies through demonstrating linkages between racism, sexual inequalities, poverty, and homelessness. As such, this work could help to contextualize the homelessness of many people within a broader systemic analysis. However, during the first few years I worked at the shelter, none of these efforts occurred. These possible statistical records were never considered necessary or useful to maintain until my ethnographic engagement helped produce new thinking and practices. In fact, as I discuss later in the text, increased collaborative efforts between a wide segment of social-justice organizations working on both decreasing poverty and structural racial inequality developed once I began to compile such data.

I began to record the data on the employment of shelter guests in 1994. This information documents over one-third of those staying at the shelter working for near minimum wage in food services or retail trade and unable to afford local rents. These data were never worth documenting or compiling and were never used in public presentations and grants because they did not fit within the dominant understandings guiding shelter practices. Even when I urged staff and policy makers to contemplate why so many working poor could not afford housing in the city, the stories of working homeless people were rarely contextualized within an analysis of local labor-market and housing conditions. Instead, these employment data were read as evidence of the need for treatment of individualized homeless people through job training. Their inability to obtain decent pay was understood as being caused by inadequacies within the homeless person, not the result of tactical business decisions.

Examining local employment conditions could offer data detailing the declining wages paid to local workers as unionized manufacturing jobs are replaced by low-paying food- and retail-trade jobs throughout the region. Such an analysis might lead to focusing staff and guest efforts on strategizing about how to alter those conditions so that the working poor could afford a place to live, building coalitions between labor and social justice activists locally, organizing for decent pay and labor conditions in local jobs, challenging dominant perceptions about homeless people, or ensuring housing as a basic right for all people. All of these actions were eventually taken in Northampton to confront the material and discursive processes creating homelessness, but only after much work transforming local practices away from a focus on individual pathology.

Record-keeping techniques have the power to reinforce or refute dominant perceptions about "the homeless" and, thus, to influence both the formulation of social policy and how average people understand homelessness. Shelter statistics are often limited representations based upon dominant "knowledge" about homelessness. They are used as mechanisms of detecting the presumed individual and group pathologies within the client. As such, these statistical representations function to construct "the homeless" as deviant and in need of professional reform. More systemic resistance efforts remain largely silenced.

The "type" of person one is forms both a central component of a person's identity and underlies others expectations, hopes, fears and attitudes about that person. The particular discursive languages and practices operating daily within the homeless sheltering industry focus homeless people's attention on their selves. Through routine practices of detecting and treating pathology, statistical record keeping, maintaining case histories, and self-help efforts, a homeless person becomes a subject who was inclined to be homeless because of something within the self.

Given these dynamics, it is hardly surprising that there are very few large-scale collective resistance struggles by homeless people against economic or racial inequality and housing policies. Subjectivities are created through the widespread languages of self-empowerment and self-improvement and practices of diagnosing and treating disorders within individuals. The discursive languages and practices within the sheltering industry make up people who self-govern. Self-blaming and self-governing subjects who are rewarded for looking within their selves for the solution to their individual homelessness can scarcely be expected to spend time on resisting systemic issues. But not everyone willingly complies with such practices. The next chapter explores the resistance efforts of the non-compliant, "difficult" shelter guest in more detail.

CHAPTER 4

The Non-Compliant Homeless: Ariel's Story

ARIEL: *"I think people try to separate themselves from homelessness so they feel safe. Instead of trying to identify with those people, they try to say how they are different and that homeless people are 'like that' as though there is some common denominator among homeless people."*

I first met Ariel, a white woman in her early 50s, when she came to the Grove Street Inn in May 1993. She had been living at a local rooming house for the previous three years but was no longer able to secure enough house-cleaning jobs to pay her rent. In this chapter, I explore her interactions with the shelter staff to demonstrate in more detail resistance by a person who did not comply with the medicalization of her homelessness. To understand the significance of Ariel's story, it is important to consider how the strategies undertaken were constrained both by dominant discursive conditions and by the material conditions within which these struggles were situated. What possible strategies and tactics for responding to homelessness were silenced by the focus on diagnosing and treating Ariel's perceived deviance?

Reading Mental Illness

Shortly after she entered the shelter, various staff members began trying to help Ariel through formal counseling, surveillance of her daily behavior, case management interviews, and informal discussions. As with many homeless people I met, Ariel was full of self-blame and was distraught when she came to the shelter. I asked her why she thought she was homeless. "I've always thought it's something inside of me that attracts it." Feeling that she had been a failure in life, she believed she "would never be the person I was meant to be."

"Sometimes I don't feel anything anymore. I know my emotions are different than if I had been a naturalist like I've always wanted. I really need to work with nature. I'd like to help establish migratory paths or something like that. I know that the next time I get some place to live that I can work from and someone can depend on me, that I'm going to do some volunteer work at the conservation area. Now, I feel like the other volunteers will leave because they wouldn't want to work with me because I feel too critical of myself."

Ariel was also quite angry about her situation. As she put it a year later, "I didn't know what to do with this anger, so I blamed myself." One example of this self-blame comes through in Ariel's explanation for why she was unable to find adequate work: "I believe there are several reasons why I have had very little work for years. I believe it's partly because a lot of people are uncomfortable making eye contact with me because of my weak eyes and can hardly stand to look at me at all. Most people believe that since my own life has been torn apart for so long, that I must destroy it myself and that I would be destructive in their place of work."

Her feelings of anguish would often manifest in Ariel losing her patience with a fellow shelter guest, becoming distraught over her situation, crying disturbingly often, and feeling scattered and unable to concentrate. She was clearly in a great deal of emotional pain. Unfortunately, this self-blame was often reinforced by the well-intentioned efforts of shelter staff.

Ariel's emotions and conduct were seen as evidence of mental illness by the many shelter staff. She was characterized as "unsafe," "very high need," "emotionally distraught," and "clinically depressed." All of the staff felt sorry for Ariel and wanted to help her as best they could. One staff member in particular, Ann, was quite struck by Ariel's life history and wanted to do all she could to help her. She urged the rest of the staff to extend Ariel's initial stay at the shelter to give us the opportunity to alter the course of Ariel's life through working intensely with her.

In this effort to help her, most staff felt we needed to discover what had made her turn out the way she had. This proved difficult at first. She did not use alcohol or drugs, except "for an occasional chocolate bar." She came across as an articulate, caring, and intelligent person. Despite never managing to pursue higher education, Ariel was extremely well read and knowledgeable on a range of topics. None of the standard diagnoses of substance abuse, mental incompetence, or mental illness appeared to apply. Staff would have to probe deeper into Ariel's life to successfully diagnose what was causing her poverty and homelessness.

After completing high school in the Midwest, Ariel worked in a variety of jobs before leaving for the West Coast. She often described her experience in Los Angeles as the most stable period of her life: "I had no problem getting a job when I was younger. Up until I was 40 and moved to the East Coast, I could always find work and support myself. I enjoyed working in a lawyer's office in California doing filing and being a receptionist. I was living in a building where several other young women lived and we really enjoyed each other's company. Then the building was sold, though, and we all had to get out. We said we'd stay in touch, but everyone moved to different parts of the city and we never did. Soon after that, I moved to the East Coast and I've had a hard time ever since."

Staff working with Ariel used this information to argue that at one point she was able to support herself. They determined that something traumatic must have happened right before this move to the East Coast. She must be suffering from some form of PTSD. Although no staff had evidence of any "trauma" in her life, except that of being homeless, it was assumed that PTSD must be the explanation for her homelessness. This was often a topic of "counseling" discussions. A staff member would try to help Ariel recall what had transpired in the hope that she could break down her denial and begin to "recover."

Few staff members acknowledged that her inability to find suitable work stemmed in part from the fact that Ariel was aging and the economy was changing. Most of the jobs Ariel had held as a younger woman involved clerical work in an office. During the 1980s, computers became commonplace in offices, displacing many clerical workers. Neither Ariel nor shelter staff showed that they understood that it is easier for a younger woman to be hired for secretarial work or that the nature of office work shifted with the introduction of computers. Instead, she was diagnosed with a mental health disorder within her self, resulting in her no longer being able to find employment.

Further evidence of Ariel's mental-health "disorder" was gathered from suggestions she frequently submitted for improved shelter practices. Unlike most people in the shelter, Ariel would often convey her thoughts to the director about improvements that could be made. Her suggested improvements ranged from advice about how to assist with housing searches to nutritional recommendations for shelter meals to systems for ensuring the kitchen was adequately cleaned. She always tried to be considerate and expressed her appreciation for the shelter while making these suggestions. However, as with Raymond, Ariel's efforts to give her advice and best intentions were deflected and portrayed by some staff as her being difficult and "providing an excuse to not focus on her issues."

Ariel explained, "I wrote a note asking, for example, if it could be established to save plates [of food] for people who were working late. I remember a fellow who was working 12 hours each day and riding a bicycle to work and I think the shelter needs to be geared, or at least have some leeway, so that this guy could at least get to eat when he comes in [according to shelter rules, the kitchen was closed after 10:00 each night]. Some staff said though, 'this is a shelter and you have to accept that these are the rules. You need to live by them and the kitchen closes at ten.' I don't like to hear that."

Vin: "So, you wrote down a suggestion and what happened?"

Ariel: "It wasn't mentioned. Nothing. It must have been filed and I thought she [Donna] must have been busy and had it filed, but nothing ever happened."

Ariel went on to explain: "I used to believe that the squeaky wheel gets the grease, but now I've learned that sometimes it gets replaced. That's one lesson I've learned in life. I've learned that those people running most shelters don't care about people at all. It's not like here where you and Donna care about those staying here and sometimes care too much. Like that night Donna was out in the rainstorm on the railroad tracks looking for someone who used to stay here. But, at most shelters, you have to keep quiet or you'll get punished."

Vin: "That happens here too. You're portrayed as being difficult."

Ariel: "Right. I'm not cooperating."

The problem was not only that Ariel was not cooperating. Her questioning of routine staff practices was portrayed as evidence of a mental illness and her unwillingness to work on the issues contributing to her individual homelessness. Staff members explained that they did not respond to her suggestions because they did not want to "encourage her denial."

Mandating Compliance/Marginalizing Resistance

ARIEL: *"Some people see homeless people as a problem that you need to hide or cure instead of as seeing the people as being fellow human beings who don't have enough money to get a place to live."*

During July 1993, some of the staff developed a treatment plan to resolve Ariel's homelessness. The first suggestion was to get Ariel into counseling and on anti-depressant medications. When she dismissed this strategy, a second plan was devised to get Ariel social security disability income (SSI) through being declared disabled. Ariel wanted nothing to do with that either. Staff frequently articulated a frustration that Ariel was being "difficult to work with" because she would not acknowledge her mental-health issues. Ariel, however, argued both that she would be lying if she went along and that doing so would cause her to lose even more self esteem.

Staff at the shelter continued to advocate the SSI plan. She was routinely called into the office for counseling sessions. These discussions consisted of the well-meaning staff member attempting to point out to Ariel how she was unable to care for herself. She was told that she needed to be declared disabled if she was to find housing. When she refused to apply for disability coverage, she was denied a further extension at the shelter. As a result of her resistance against these practices, Ariel spent August through December struggling for survival while living on the streets.

I asked Ariel to describe her feelings about how the staff worked with her during this period. Ariel stated, "Well, the person I worked with at Grove

Street was Ann and Ann is a totally different temperament than me. We are total opposites. One time I was telling Ann that she had hurt my feelings. Ann kept telling me I was offensive. I thought, 'What?' But, it was because I wasn't doing what she wanted by applying for SSI. And, I like Ann. She cares. She cares about women's's issues. And then there's other staff like Linda who'd be condescending and I'd tell her. Then she'd do it again and I'd feel like, is it just that this takes time?"

Vin: "How was she condescending?"

Ariel: "She'd talk to me like I was three."

Vin: "Like she knows what's best for you?"

Ariel: "Yeah, like when we were working in the garden. It wasn't like two women working together in the garden. She was the one who knew what was right and I was like a child who didn't have anything to contribute."

Vin: "Yeah, if, in your mind, you are supposed to be there as the miracle worker who will save these people or make them better, then that staff ends up treating the homeless person bad when their efforts don't work. Ann even said that this summer. She said that she thought she was supposed to save everybody and fix them and then she'd get mad at them and get mad at herself and it wouldn't do anyone any good."

Ariel: "Humm. It was like she was looking for results whenever she would try to help me with something. I said one time, 'Why is it that whenever we talk it's about what's wrong with me?' I think temperament really has a lot to do with it. Like, Ann would be kind one moment and then she would glare at me or call me offensive."

Ariel described her resistance to applying for disability. "I tell Elizabeth when I have thought about applying for SSI, even telling the truth, even my way of applying which would be simply saying that 'I'm not disabled, I just simply don't have any money, so send it please.' It's not my fault where you have this system where you have to be disabled to have some money. But, I explain that the way I feel about it is that once I have applied, it will be permanent and I'd be a failure. Not only would I have failed to be the person I was meant to be, which I've already lost faith in the idea that I'll ever be that person years ago, but I'd always be a failure within my self because I gave up on my self. I want to accomplish something and not just take. It seems like I'm always trying to get a job or a place to live. I don't have time to really do what I value and really have close friends or do something good. I mean, I don't want to get a job just so I can buy things.

"I decided a long time ago that I didn't want to be a success unless I could be strong, noble, wise, and loving. I don't want to be strong unless I'm right first. I remember when I was a little girl reading about World War II and some people decided they wanted to build bombs and kill people and they succeeded. They were successful. I never wanted to be successful if that's what it means. I need to establish my values and live in harmony with them so I can respect my self."

Instead of respecting these values, most shelter staff looked at her as being "unrealistic." It was nice to have such values, but when sticking to them resulted in losing privilege it was understood and portrayed as pathological. Ariel was mentally ill because she put her values before her personal income or even being housed. Rather than supporting this trait, most shelter staff viewed it as further evidence of a disorder needing to be normalized through therapy and medication if Ariel was ever to be housed. The goal of most staff members became to reform Ariel so she could cope with a society based on competition, individual success, inequality, and a lack of concern for nature. They explained that this was unfortunate, but it was the only way to "help" her. The function of the sheltering industry remains to "fix" the homeless and not to alter or contest cultural and socio-economic conditions contributing to the existence of homelessness.

Ariel never denied that she was upset. It would be clear to anyone who met Ariel at this time that she was far from happy. What she resented was an implication that her feeling angry and sad over being homeless was evidence of mental illness that had caused her homelessness. She stated, "Doesn't it seem that the rational reaction is to be depressed when you find yourself in a shelter? I would think it would be more of a sign of mental illness if you accepted being here."

Ariel became even more upset by the efforts to convince her that she was mentally ill. "I need people to say encouraging things. I need people that I believe in and that I feel believe in me. I need to feel that someone believes in me. I don't need someone to tell me that I'm going to freeze to death or lose my fingers and toes unless I say I'm disabled. I need someone to pull me up."

Vin: "You have to say that you're disabled or …."

Ariel: "Or, you can't stay anywhere. Or, you can't stay here, you can't stay there, you can't stay anywhere. I say, fine. Well, I'll just turn to the Creator again. I'm basically spiritual. I'm not basically intellectual. But, when I say that, Harry [the shelter director at the time] says I'm confusing him."

Vin: "Right, and he has the power to decide that your concept of the Creator is weird and wrong and his is right."

Ariel: "Then the feedback I get is 'well, you want us to take care of you.' No, I don't. But, I feel that I have a right to be indoors even if I haven't accomplished much."

What Ariel wanted was assistance with finding housing and employment. During August 1993, several staff reluctantly worked with Ariel on alternatives to getting social security. Ann suggested that she move to a commune in Tennessee, but Ariel was reluctant to leave the area and give up the few friends that she had made. Elizabeth helped her with re-writing her résumé and a cover letter. Ariel felt that she needed to figure out how to explain to potential employers the large gaps in her recent employment history. Ann discussed the idea of helping Ariel with making an ad in the paper for house-work or putting up signs in strategic locations around town. Throughout all of these efforts, however, staff continued to focus daily on convincing Ariel to apply for SSI. They saw it as the only realistic option she had to secure a place to live.

Finally, in early September, Harry and Donna decided that she would have to leave the shelter at the end of the month. This was presented at the staff meeting as the only option available. The hope was that living on the street would force her to "accept our help." The view was voiced that "maybe she's one of those people who have to hit rock-bottom before they are ready to come up." She was given the option of applying for social security disability insurance and subsidized housing.

What no staff would admit was that, even if Ariel was declared disabled and did begin receiving SSI, there was no guarantee that she would then be housed. She would only receive approximately $450 each month, which isn't enough to pay rent anywhere except for a rooming-house room. Waiting lists for subsidized apartments or Section 8 certificates extend for several years. If Ariel did give in, her only real housing option would be to live in poverty in a rooming house. She refused that option.

Despite my daily pleas in staff meetings, log notes, and discussions with other staff, Ariel was kicked out of the shelter because "she was being dif-ficult." "Being difficult" was defined as not applying for social security dis-ability insurance by claiming a mental health disability. Staff were frustrated by not knowing how to resolve her homelessness and from their viewpoint social security was the only option. Ariel said goodbye and that she was sorry that Ann, Donna, and Harry were so angry with her. She said she wished she could make them happier, but she needed to do what she thought best. On October 3, she left the shelter and began living outside.

Ariel called me at the shelter three weeks later. I was still hoping to change the minds of other staff members so that Ariel could return. Ariel was trying everything she could to find work or a place to live, but with no luck. "I keep thinking to myself that there is something I haven't thought of or tried. There must be. There must be something that I'm doing wrong." Beds occasionally became available at the shelter throughout this period of time, but she was not allowed to sleep inside because she needed to "face reality."

Ariel described to me how she was struggling to survive during this time. I said, "You were staying in a laundry for awhile."

Ariel: "Yeah, I was sitting there in a chair and putting my feet up. So, that was nice because I was able to get some sleep. I wasn't afraid or anything. I knew no harm was going to come to me there, but now someone complained and I can't stay there any longer."

Vin: "There's really no place that's open 24 hours."

Ariel: "Except for stores where you have to buy something. If I had money to buy something, I'd get a place to live."

Vin: "I wonder where other people stay because there's a lot of people I know who are staying outside now."

Ariel: "Really, I'm the only one I know of and I've been walking around thinking I must be doing something wrong with me if I'm the only one."

Vin: "So, at this point, you need to find some place to live. That's your goal."

Ariel: "I have a lot of ability. All I need is a place to stay and I'd buy my own food. There must be somebody around who needs a free live-in house-keeper. There must be. Another thing I've been thinking is that maybe people are reluctant to hire someone without insurance. I found something at the state employment office about insurance paid for by the federal government which I'm applying for. Maybe I'd get more work if I could get some insurance. So, that could be one solution. That could be part of the reason why I can't even barter for a place."

After Ariel's first night on the street, Harry offered her the option of a room at a nearby program for mentally ill homeless people. He hoped that the one night outside would have convinced her to be more cooperative. No staff enjoyed knowing Ariel was living outside, but forcing her to do so was represented as the only way to "help" her. The hardship of living on the streets was portrayed as a treatment tool in that it would force Ariel to cooperate with efforts to treat the diagnosed deviancy. Ariel refused Harry's offer when she found out that it was funded by the Department of Mental Health for home-less people with documented mental illnesses. As a condition of living there she would have to apply for SSI. She survived outside from October through mid-December when the seasonal guilt of Christmas and the extreme cold led enough staff to reconsider and let her move back into the shelter.

After Ariel was allowed to return to the shelter, I asked her about her emotions and the experience of being forced to "hit bottom": "Why do you think Ann and Donna and everyone tried to convince you to get on SSI?"

Ariel: "I don't know. I feel like I trust their attitude toward me. I think it's that they don't know what else they, personally, can do. What else they can do."

Vin: "That's what I think too."

Ariel: "I know that the one thing I kept saying to them was that I needed to believe in myself or I didn't need to live at all. I need some people to believe in me. Instead of saying that you're going to end up under a bridge. It seems that over the years there have been quite a few of these social workers and welfare in different states and they were always saying, 'you're going to end up....' It was always something down and dire. Like, 'you're going to end up a bag lady.' So, I said to Donna, 'I need encouragement.' I need to believe in myself. I need people who are in a position to talk to me at all to encourage me to believe in myself. Not say, 'what are you going to do when it gets cold?' How the hell should I know what I'm going to do? I'm not in a position to decide anything!"

Vin: "Right, you're not in a position with very many choices. What choices you do have aren't very good."

Ariel: "Right, I need someone to encourage me about new options. They say, well, there aren't many options and I say the Creator knows of options that we might not know anything about and no-one is asking the Creator. I say I need people to say a prayer for me and be more optimistic than I am when I can't be very optimistic and believe in the value of my capacity to love when I'm not believing in it. Believe in the value of my qualities when I'm not believing in that and encourage me in that. That's what I need. I need people to believe in the value of my qualities and what I can do to be part of something good."

Vin: "So, when things all seem to be falling apart, you don't need someone making you feel worse about yourself?"

Ariel: "Yeah, they say, there's something wrong with you so you should go on SSI because there's something permanently wrong with you. Just give up and go on SSI. Forget it."

Vin: "So, you think when Ann's doing her 'reality check' that she's helping to create a reality?"

Ariel: "Exactly. The word reality really just means whatever the person's concept and perception is at the time. The real reality is the Creator of the universe's reality. I really used to just hate myself and be furious with myself for not ever having things work out. I need to exercise more faith in the creator and not be so anxious and blaming of myself. All that kind of stuff, you know."

As soon as Ariel moved back into the shelter, the efforts to get her to be declared mentally ill began anew. Almost daily meetings occurred in the staff office. By early January, shelter staff were threatening to kick her back out to the streets if she didn't work with them. The shelter director gave her three options. She could go to a transitional shelter in Greenfield, but she did not want that option because it included applying for disability and all of her house-cleaning work 20 miles away with no easy bus service between them. As a second option, she could go to a newly opened shelter even farther away, which would mean that she could not continue her work. Finally, Ariel could apply for SSI and go to a mental-health program.

For Ariel, none of these was a good option. She eventually went to the new shelter until it closed on May 1, 1995. It was better than freezing to death that winter. While living in that shelter, Ariel would often commute the 25 miles daily by bus to Northampton in an effort to look for work. This involved searching the local paper, searching for jobs at the Department of Employment and Training office, and placing flyers around the town.

In May, Ariel was allowed to return to Grove Street. She again faced pressure to apply for SSI, stop "being so self-defeating," and "be realistic." I attempted in staff meetings to reframe the discussions and to get us to stop looking at what was wrong with Ariel and instead look at what was wrong with a society that does not provide someone like Ariel with housing or the ability to support herself. However, this was seen as impractical and unrealistic.

Ann was the staff person who primarily worked on enforcing this plan. A year later I asked Ann, "Think back about a year and a half ago. What else could we have offered Ariel? What could be done with someone who is in a position like she is? How did it feel being in your position in the day program and feeling that you have to work with her?"

Ann responded, "Well, I remember when I did work with Ariel. Eventually, I got to the point of real frustration. I think that since then and since like a couple of conversations at staff meetings that I've been to more recently where we've been talking about what's going on with Ariel and how to be supportive of her, that, we were looking at things through our eyes and through, sort of, the lens of normalizing or mainstreaming people."

My future wife, Sarah, began to volunteer at the shelter during this time and became close to Ariel. Sarah and Ariel would spend long hours in the kitchen discussing nutrition, recycling, vegetarian cooking, and similar common interests. During this time, I too began to spend more time just talking with Ariel. As we spent long evenings discussing a wide range of topics, I began to understand Ariel as a deep-thinking, compassionate, and kind human being instead of as simply a homeless person whom it was my job to normalize. We became closer and more trusting as I began to deeply question shelter practices aimed at pathologizing her. I began to advocate more for trying to be more supportive and not reinforcing her already existing self-blame.

Unfortunately for Ariel, my wedding was scheduled for June 25. I left on June 23 and went on a one-month honeymoon. A day later she was told that she would have to leave in 30 days. From all accounts, this was a month of pure hell for both staff and Ariel. Gloria, Donna, and Ann put renewed pressure on her, trying to force her to "deal with reality," doing "reality checks" with her, and it just drove her to become more and more resistant and angry with the staff. I was not there either to advocate for her with other staff or to be an outlet for her to discuss her plans and interactions with staff. She got into a bitter argument with Gloria the day before I came back to work and was once again banished to the streets for being difficult and not willing to work with staff.

Sarah and I met Ariel for lunch a few weeks later. As we talked about her situation, I said that I wanted to know if she wanted to come back and if I should bother to try to get her let back into the house. Ariel did not want to come back. She asked me, "Sometimes people on staff just act on their emotions and not on how the rules are. They might be having a bad night and start giving people warnings when they normally wouldn't. Do you think that's what happened when Gloria came up on Saturday morning and told me I had to leave? I hadn't gotten any warnings or anything."

Vin: "Yep, she certainly does that. She seems to fear some people staying there and gets very angry when you don't give her the respect she thinks she deserves. When they don't, in her mind, she gets angry and becomes confrontational."

Ariel: "Yeah, you know the reason why I left was that I really didn't trust her attitude and I felt that a few minutes later she was going to come up and say that the police were going to be there. That's why I left. I felt that was what she'd do. She'd go downstairs and call the police to throw me out if I didn't leave. And that's the only reason why I left and I shouldn't have. I should have told her that I'm not leaving until Hannah or Donna tell me I have to leave. I was just going to be there until Tuesday anyway, but still. That's how I felt at the time. I was just so tired of it all. You know, I didn't want it to come to that."

Vin: "Muriel [another shelter guest who was struggling against similar efforts to "treat" her] was very proud of you though. That was the day after I came back from vacation. She came and told me that story and said how you walked out with dignity rather than resorting to fighting with Gloria."

Ariel continued recounting this experience with a great deal of sorrow and regret in her voice. "I just didn't have the right frame of mind for the whole situation. I really didn't trust her. I thought she'd call the police. I told Donna that I feel differently about the house because of the way I left and that I wasn't reinstated. Now, I don't ever want to go back there."

Vin: "So, you didn't want to risk losing the positive relationships that you had developed there with some staff and felt that the safest way would be to just leave."

Ariel: "Yeah, I was just so tired of it all though. I think I'm happier living outside than constantly being told I'm a failure and disabled and that I need to apply for SSI. So, maybe it wasn't so bad. When I left Grove Street and didn't have any place to sleep, I told Donna, 'I feel better, something's wrong with the house. I've been without a place to stay for over a week and I feel better.' It wasn't how I wanted to feel. It's just how I felt."

Ariel tried to live in shelters in nearby cities during the following weeks, but found them unsafe and impossible because she was going hungry. They would primarily serve meat and not allow her to cook or bring her own food. "In Springfield, you have to go across the bridge to the nearest grocery store every time you want to eat. You couldn't even bring two slices of cheese in there. If you don't want to eat meat or pasta, there are lots of nights when you just have to go hungry in many shelters." Ariel was kicked out of the other shelter for breaking the rules by trying to make a cheese sandwich with a "weapon" (a butter knife). She soon came back to Northampton to live on the streets.

Sarah and I met Ariel in Amherst one afternoon during this period while she was living outside and talked about her plans and feelings. At that point, she was starting to feel like giving up and applying for SSI if it meant that she could live inside again.

Ariel: "My hands and feet are hurting so much from a lack of sleep and proper nutrition that I told Elizabeth that I'm about ready to give up and apply for SSI. If I do, though, I will tell them the truth that I did this, I worked at that, I'm strong in these ways. Tell them the truth. I'm not mentally disabled. Don't call me mentally disabled. Make it a loan if you want to. Nobody has to know. Just make it a loan and I'll pay it back. Just don't declare me mentally disabled. How am I supposed to get a job? You know, you go on SSI and people find that out. How are you ever going to get a job when you're obviously not physically disabled? Then you're obviously mentally disabled and they'll figure you go off all the time. They can't tell by looking at you or talking to you. They get scared that there must be something within you that goes off at times. Why would they want to hire you then?"

Vin: "But, I think people feel that there has to be something wrong with the person if you're homeless."

Ariel: "Yeah, nobody wants you around. Why don't you have a place to live?"

Vin: "Or, there are jobs at McDonalds. Why don't you just get a job at McDonalds?"

Ariel: "Sometimes when you've already sat in McDonalds in the middle of the night or washed up in their bathroom you know they're not going to hire you then. It's hard for people who don't live like this to understand."

Vin: "Even if you worked in a place like that, you can't get enough to live with the wages they pay."

Ariel: "With the pay, I couldn't even afford to buy their food. I'd rather starve than eat their food. You're probably better off not eating anything than eat their food. Then there are other jobs that I could probably get, but when you don't have a place to live you can't keep yourself clean enough. It's all I can do to sneak into a bathroom and spend a half an hour. By the time you get your stuff out and all your clothes off, the restaurant or store is ready to kick you out."

Vin: "So, you need a place to live first."

Ariel: "Yes. You can't work at a job where you get dirty because you can't ever get yourself clean when you're living outside. I think some of the staff at the house, or anybody, would say, 'Well, why do you keep living like this?' and I say, 'Well the alternative is to commit suicide and I'm not going to commit suicide. The alternative to [committing suicide is that] I'm willing to walk around with no place to live because I have no place to live. I'm willing to walk around with no place to stay because I have no place to stay. Because I'm willing to keep on living that's why. I'm willing to walk around all night or sit up in stop and shop because I'm not willing to jump off a bridge. Those are my options.'"

Vin: "And you think that getting SSI so you can have a little room in some rooming house wouldn't be living, it would be giving up?"

Ariel: "Oh, I'm not going to lie. I'm going to tell them the truth. They better not declare me mentally disabled. Either they're not going to send me the check or they're going to send it to me on my terms. I will have access to the records and if they do declare me mentally disabled, I will not accept their check. I am not mentally disabled, but I do need money to get a place to live or I need to barter. [laughing] If a psychiatrist needs a housekeeper and a couch in the rec room, that would work out fine."

Vin: "But, you can only get social security by having a mental or physical disability. The thinking is that if you don't have one of those, you should be able to make it on your own."

Ariel: "Right, so why don't they just work out a loan and for people who really cannot work and compete in the business world, they can get a check and they should also figure out some way they can get some education or learn how to do something to contribute to the world."

Vin: "It seems that the staff here seems to get mad at the person when we can't come up with the easy solution for somebody."

Ariel: "I think so. I think that they're seeing me as a problem. I say, well just say a prayer for me. I didn't do anything perfectly, but then there are an awful lot of businesses that are closing. I was renting a room and I was doing housework and maybe I didn't know enough. I was willing to do a lot of different things, but I just didn't get enough work to hang onto my room. That doesn't mean I'm mentally ill. I'm not mentally ill. I just can't find enough work. There's alot of different jobs that I've applied for. I just can't find work."

Vin: "Well, you've worked for many years and were able to support yourself right?"

Ariel: "Yeah, from when I was 18 on my own until I was 40, I always managed. I always took care of myself and worked. But, it's easier when you're younger. I think that it definitely has to do with the economy now. It's not just me. I'm not the only one who can't support themself now."

Vin: "But, then we think we can't change the economy."

Ariel: "Exactly, it's 'we can't change the economy, so we better change you.'"

Ariel was resisting the bio-medical discourse operating in the shelter. Yet her choices were clearly constrained. She could cooperate with the staff plan by applying for SSI or she could live outside trying to survive on her own. Her spiritual faith and need to believe in her own abilities were understood by staff as irrational evidence of a mental-health disorder. In this search for diagnosing and treating disorders within individual homeless subjects, the possibilities of staff and guests working collectively to challenge structural inequities were silenced. Possible staff and guest practices of collectively working to challenge racial or economic inequality were far removed from the routine relationship between staff and guests, where staff worked to treat pathologies within homeless people. Ariel understood that, but believed it came down to "the creator."

Ariel: "It is possible for us to have a healthy country where everyone can have a good job. It is possible. The creator can help us do that. People need to keep thinking that way instead of just accepting that the economy is bad."

Vin: "Right, and then accepting that people are going to be homeless and staff need to help people cope with a bad economy. If we thought we could have a healthy country and worked toward that, all of our efforts might be different."

Ariel: "Exactly. It doesn't do anyone any good to think I am doomed or to accept that this is how things will always be."

Vin: "Right, that's what seems weird to me. That somehow it's become normal now for people to accept having people living in the streets or in shelters. It's like, we don't have to do anything about it because it's normal. That's just how it is. How does it become acceptable to step over another person who has to sleep outside? It's crazy."

Ariel: "Yeah, I think that people are getting to the point where they say, that's just how life is, that it's just normal. I say, no, that's lack of life. That doesn't have to be the way it is. The creator wants everyone to be able to become the person they were meant to be. To be able to take care of their spiritual well-being, their intellectual well-being, their emotional well-being, their physical well-being simultaneously. And also take care of the planet. You know. And, it's possible. But, people need to think that way and they need to keep caring and keep trying. I keep saying it's going to take forever because I'll never give up."

As Ariel was struggling to survive living on the streets and in other shelters, she would call me weekly at the shelter to talk. I explained how I admired her courage and dignity and was trying my best to engage with the staff at the shelter in an analysis of our routine practices so that staff wouldn't treat other people the same way. Ariel explained how difficult it was to maintain her dignity and courage while living on the streets.

During this period, our relationship moved somewhat further away from the largely accepted dichotomous nature of shelter staff and client. I gave Ariel copies of academic papers that I had presented at conferences and had based partly on her experiences. The shelter staff had begun to use these papers as entry points for examining our case management practices, mission, and rules. Ariel would send me newspaper and magazine articles about homelessness which she thought might help me with my work.

During this same period, an old friend of mine who had just moved to the area was giving free evening lectures on natural medicine in an effort to establish his naturopathic doctor's practice. Sharing Ariel's interest in natural remedies, I would drive her to the lectures. Although I felt awful as I dropped her off at bus stops knowing that she had no place to spend the night after the lectures, Ariel described these affirming events as fundamental to her beginning to feel better about herself: "I need to know that people value me as a person and I can have friends. This wasn't about taking care of me or trying to tell me how I should live. By supporting what I was interested in and treating me like an equal, it helped me gain some self respect back." Later, when Sarah's father suffered a serious head injury, Ariel researched nutritional remedies and sent us the information.

Unfortunately, in the summer of 1995 Ariel was still homeless and needed to return to the shelter. This stay was quite different, however. The effort wasn't solely on how to fix her. Rather, Leopoldina (a newer staff member who became very critical of shelter rhetoric and practice through our discussions) and I allowed her to be angry, caring, and free to express her feelings. As Leopoldina explained, "I like to work with the angry people and they like to work with me. Look at Ariel. Ariel got to be angry in her last stay. Damn angry and she was wise to be angry. And she went out having relationships. People were seeing her as a wise and wonderful woman which she deserved to be recognized as."

Leopoldina was quite adamant that we consider Ariel's situation as an older, single, working-class woman whose homelessness and poverty were the result of social policy and economic decisions, not individual deviancy. When staff attempted to control her in prescribed efforts to reform and normalize her self, Leopoldina and I defended Ariel's rights. Ariel felt she had more support and, consequently, also spoke up when staff attempted to control and manage her. I asked Ariel about this altered approach.

Vin: "You say that you used to be really angry at yourself and not liking yourself up until the last year. Why do you think that has changed?"

Ariel: "Leopoldina has made a huge difference because of who she is. Because I talk to her a lot and she likes me. I always enjoyed talking with you and I trust and respect you and Leopoldina, and Donna, to some extent. That together has helped. I feel like I've developed some relationships with people who I trust and who seem to respect me and who value me. That's helped enormously. I don't feel like I just need to get my teeth fixed and move on. I felt that way when I first moved to the area. But, yeah, having you and Leopoldina and Deidre [a friend] and a few other friends has made a difference."

Vin: "It definitely seems that way. Even now compared to a year ago. You seem much happier."

Ariel: "Even though I still don't have a place to stay. Yeah. Having a roof over your head doesn't help if there are all kinds of terrible things going on under that roof."

"I used to really be very critical of myself and have a lot of anguish and unhappiness and anger, but it's gone. It's been gone for a good while now. I don't feel all that anguish. It used to be with me all the time. I should have gotten more education and developed a career, but there are people who did that who have no place to live. Even Childs toy store went out of business. I mean, excuse me. I think that as the jobs get sent overseas. I think it's part of it. There are so many banks and jewelry businesses going out of business. Even the dollar store is having a going out of business sale."

Vin: "Well, when we did that interview last year you said it was something about yourself and that you had to fix something about yourself or that you were the problem. It's so easy to think about just your self."

Ariel: "Rugged individualism. That you're supposed to take care of everything yourself. I was very much brought up with that stuff."

Vin: "If you can't make it, there is something wrong with you. You need to figure out what's wrong with you and fix that. I think that's what the staff at the shelter does and thinks. They might not say it still. They might talk about the society and stuff, but what they do is look at what's wrong with the person. You know, 'Look at Ariel. She doesn't use drugs or alcohol. It must be mental health because there's got to be something wrong with you.' It can't be that here is somebody who just can't make enough to support yourself."

Ariel: "Yeah, and like I must lose the jobs because of something I do like an inability to communicate or relate. I don't think I lose jobs because of that. I know that I've been living in very, very, very stressful situations for the last several years and it's been hard for me to be on the people's wavelength after being in the shelter or rooming house. How can you be on the wavelength of people who have this nice life and they have a home and he's a doctor and she's working in a lab and they're going to have a baby? How can I even try to keep my spirits up when I'm living in houses where people smell up the entire house with alcohol and there are constant arguments and stress? I mean, when I was living on the West Coast and had an apartment and could come back and fix myself a big salad, I had no problem keeping a job. It affects you living in all that stress."

Ariel was still intent on finding a job. She spent hours each day trying to re-write her résumé and design a cover letter that could explain to potential employers the gaps in her work history. When she got any money, she invested it in advertising to try to secure more housekeeping work. To Ariel, finding paid work was the key for her to resolve her homelessness and to become "the person I was meant to be." However, she will not accept employment out of pity or any that she does not find intellectually and spiritually rewarding: "I know what it's like to be homeless. I've done it long enough to know how to survive while retaining my sense of who I am. I know I could not work in some restaurant or hotel where they expect you to use harmful chemicals and not care about the quality of your work. I wouldn't last a week. People need to find emotional, intellectual, and spiritual meaning in what they do."

Unfortunately, there is little paid employment available that fit these criteria, especially for someone who has been in and out of homelessness for years. Therefore, this hard-working, dignified, thoughtful, and caring woman remained homeless and blamed herself for the situation. As she said, "I keep thinking to myself that there is something I haven't thought of or tried. There must be. Other people have homes. There must be something that I'm still doing wrong."

At a staff meeting that summer, Ariel came up because she had been at the shelter for 38 days. I said that I thought our options were either to kick Ariel out at 60 or 90 days or to let her stay longer without trying to reform her. Gloria said that maybe we should look into nearby intentional communities as options. Leopoldina suggested that she go with Ariel to off-campus housing [an office at the University of Massachusetts designed to help students locate housing] and look for live-in positions with a person who might be compatible with Ariel. Leopoldina also said that she thought that maybe we could pitch in to buy a position-wanted ad in the *Gazette*. No other staff wanted to try that option. Eventually, we decided to let Ariel stay longer.

In early January 1996, Ariel received a notice from the Housing Allowance Project (HAP) that her name had come up on their waiting list for a possible subsidized apartment. Elizabeth, as a social worker for the Department of Mental Health, had place Ariel's name on the waiting list for HAP years previously. Elizabeth, Leopoldina, and Donna were very excited over the prospect, but they were all worried that Ariel would "shoot herself in the foot during the interview by being difficult." I was pretty hesitant and pessimistic because she had not been certified as disabled, which was a criterion for the housing subsidy, but I decided to keep my pessimism to myself.

Ariel seemed to be keeping her options open. She didn't want to get too excited because on some level she seemed to be assuming that she wouldn't get accepted, but she really wanted to believe that she'd get her own apartment. She just didn't know what else to do. She knew that her time at the shelter was almost up and she had no other plans or money. She'd hurt her ankle slipping on ice and, having no insurance, hadn't received proper medical treatment. Therefore, she hadn't been able to work at all for the previous month and had no money.

Ariel got turned down for the HAP subsidized housing in January. The reason given was, as I expected, that she was not officially categorized as "disabled" by a physician or psychiatrist. Due to the huge number of people unable to afford local rents who apply for subsidies, one needs to be officially disabled or elderly to qualify for their housing.

As Ariel put it, "It's OK. I expected it, but I feel bad for Elizabeth because she was so excited about it." Elizabeth had originally put Ariel on the waiting list without telling Ariel a little over two years ago and was jubilant when her name finally came up for an interview. Leopoldina was excited also. Both could not imagine how Ariel could not qualify.

Ariel said to me, "I don't care that much. At this point I wouldn't want to go there because I'm tired of programs which are intent on pulling people down instead of lifting them up. I'm not going to say I'm disabled so that I can get a place to live. I'm physically able to work [her ankle injury did not count as a disability because it was a temporary injury]. That's clear to anyone. So, then, I would have to say that I'm mentally impaired and I'm not. I can think perfectly clearly."

In late February 1996, Ariel told me that she had lost one of her housekeeping jobs. One of the women that she worked for had been told by her HMO that she needed to hire a certified home health aide. In the past, the woman had been given a set amount of money each month to take care of her personal care and housekeeping costs. She then hired Ariel for 5 or 10 hours a month from that account. But without that money she couldn't afford to pay Ariel. Ariel understood that she would just have to look harder to find more work.

In March, the social-service agency that runs the shelter opened a new rooming house with all subsidized rooms paid for by HUD. I sat on the selection committee where a group of eight social-service professionals decided which 14 poor people were most worthy of being given the privilege of living in a small room in the rooming house. Over 40 people applied. Ann, who had stopped working at the shelter, and I advocated strongly for Ariel and, consequently, Ariel was chosen as one of the tenants. Her selection was fraught with difficulty, however, as I had to argue against the strenuous objections from Donna. Donna continued to stress how Ariel was mentally ill, unsafe in the kitchen, and a disruptive influence.

Ariel was very hesitant about moving into the building because she wanted her own apartment, not a rooming house. She felt that there would be problems in any rooming house because "of the type of people who live there." She foresaw a lot of theft of food, disrespectful behavior, noisy tenants, drunken behavior, and other problems. Leopoldina, Donna, and I urged her to at least look at the building and try to give it a chance. We stressed that this was a new building and it was to be tenant-managed. For that model to work, we explained, we needed tenants in the building who were as thoughtful and caring as Ariel. She consented to take a tour of the building and was excited by its condition: "It looks like a bed and breakfast. It's a shame that it has to be a rooming house because you know it will be ruined soon."

Ariel did move in because she trusted that Leopoldina and I would help manage the building, but she was not happy. As she told me, "I refuse to look at this as something to be happy about. Everyone is acting like I should be jumping up and down in joy, but it's a rooming house. I need to work to get my own apartment. As soon as you get happy and content, you get stuck and go backwards. It must be some law of human nature. It's happened so many times to me that I know I can't get too happy. I need to find work so I can get my own apartment. Living here is still like accepting charity because it is subsidized. That is still saying that I need someone to take care of me. I can take care of myself. I just need to get more work."

Her analysis was right on the mark. Most shelter staff, including myself, who had been working with Ariel for the last three years were overjoyed to see her in stable housing. It was only when she pointed out that it was still a room and she was still living on less than $100 a month that I realized that her "success" wasn't so wonderful after all.

One Wednesday a few weeks later, I stopped by the rooming house to drop off some food for ex-shelter guests living there. I was greeted at the door by Ariel and another tenant, Michael, asking me if I had read the article in yesterday's local newspaper. I said that I hadn't had a chance to yet, but I would read the copy Hannah (the administrator overseeing both the rooming house and shelter) dropped off. Hannah was very excited about the article because it spent a great deal of time showing how the tenants of the rooming house were planning on reaching out and trying to become a part of the community. Several neighbors and local businesses had been opposed to the rooming house because of the "type" of people who would be living there. The article was based largely on interviews with two tenants who had stated how everyone was working hard to improve themselves and get back on track and out of poverty. Hannah was thrilled because she thought this article might alter neighbors' views of those living in the house.

Michael and Ariel, on the other hand, were quite upset about the way the article represented those living at the rooming house. Walter, a third tenant whom I was close to from his time in the shelter, soon walked into the kitchen and also voiced his disenchantment with the sentiments expressed in the article. Michael said, "It says that everyone staying here has a physical or mental disability. That's not true at all. Maybe Walter and me have physical problems right now, but it's not most of us. And I'm starting work soon despite my medical problems. It makes it look like there's something wrong with everyone and that's why we're staying here. We live here because we can't afford any place else."

After reading the article, I said, "I see what you mean. It's saying that this is like some type of program which is going to help rehabilitate you so that you can become part of mainstream society. It's the old American Dream and meritocracy myth again."

Ariel: "Right. We don't want to live in a subsidized room, but I'm here because I can't find enough work. Articles like this are going make the neighbors fear us even more. I told Elizabeth about the story this morning and she said, 'But Ariel, you are depressed.' That was her answer."

One evening in May, I went to the rooming house to help facilitate the house meeting. As I pulled into the driveway, I noticed an ambulance and two police cars by the building. Walter and Roberto met me in the parking lot and explained that one of the tenants had overdosed on pills in a suicide attempt. This tenant had been very disruptive in the rooming house for the last few weeks. All reports were that she was using drugs and turning tricks in her room to pay for the heroin. Despite frequent complaints from the other tenants in the house, especially Ariel, there was not much Hannah could do as a landlord unless the tenant was caught with drugs in her room. Hannah and

I spoke with her on several occasions and offered help getting her back into detox or counseling, but nothing had worked very well.

Toward the end of the house meeting, the subject of the suicide attempt was raised for discussion. All of the tenants voiced their concern about the events and their fellow tenant's health, but several were also quite vocal in their feelings that she should not be allowed back in the house. Ariel said, "She just tried to take a human life upstairs. Excuse me, if she had tried to murder somebody else in the house, would she be allowed back here? I hope not. I do not want to be living next door to someone who is trying to take a human life."

Hannah defended her decision: "She asked for help and is getting some help right now." Another guest voiced his feeling that she was going to the hospital and would probably be held there for a few weeks while she had some counseling. He said that he thought it would be fine to let her back after such a stay in the hospital. Hannah agreed with this sentiment. Ariel, Roberto, Walter, and other tenants were all still quite upset by the prospect of her returning. Ariel pointed out that "she needs help. She has been trying to kill herself for the last several weeks with drugs, having men come to her room, and now this. She needs more help than she can get here. If she comes back, it's only a matter of time before she tries it again. We should not have to live like this. I just need to move out of here as soon as possible."

Hannah told me the next day that Ariel had called her at home at midnight because the woman was released from Emergency Services and was back in the house. Hannah said that she was upset both at the hospital for releasing her and at Ariel for responding in the manner she did: "She was hysterical on the phone, saying, 'you promised she'd be gone for three weeks.' It was completely inappropriate."

Hannah said that she had spoken with Elizabeth about Ariel's behavior. Elizabeth immediately resorted to a mental-health diagnosis. She suggested to Hannah to have Ariel call Emergency Services, not, however, to complain about their treatment of the woman who was discharged four hours after attempting suicide, but, rather, to ask for mental health help herself. "This must have triggered some suppressed memory from her [Ariel's] past and so maybe this will be good because it will push her to finally confront some of these issues." Hannah took this advice. No matter what her motive, Ariel's behavior was always heard stereotypically. Pathologizing Ariel was easier than to confront an inadequate health-care system.

Ariel's reluctance to live next door to someone who was selling her body for drug money and attempting suicide was turned into evidence of her own individual disorder. After four years and all of my efforts to challenge shelter workers to think differently about Ariel and homelessness, this incident was

simply understood by some staff and administrators as more evidence of a
mental-health problem within Ariel.

Ariel was even more upset after her conversations with Elizabeth
and Hannah. She called Leopoldina at the shelter and was relieved when
Leopoldina let her know that her anger was very justified. The individualized
mental-disorder model of looking at the world of the housed and the homeless was so dominant for Elizabeth and Hannah that it had become routine.
Ariel, Leopoldina, and I wondered how Elizabeth and Hannah would react if
they had to live under those conditions, but we agreed that these professional
workers in the homelessness industry would not be able to fathom living in
a rooming house because they are "normal," mentally fit Americans. Thus,
they seem incapable of seeing themselves in the same position.

I asked Leopoldina, "What do you think about what happened when the
woman living next door to her [Ariel] tried to commit suicide and Ariel got
very mad that she was back from the hospital three hours later?"

Leopoldina: "She called me three days later. She hadn't called me in
months. She was seeking me to talk to. She asked, 'Why the hell did Hannah
sick Elizabeth on me, when all I did was ...,' and she explained what happened.
I said 'Look, I was there the next day and I was rip shit too that they had let out
this woman who had clearly tried to kill herself without helping her.' I didn't
get into what time she [Ariel] called Hannah and that she had screamed at her,
but I said, 'You have every right to be pissed. It was an insane, immoral way of
handling it.' No, I wouldn't have sicked a mental health worker on Ariel."

Vin: "Hannah told me that Elizabeth suggested that she tell Ariel to call
Emergency Services and get help for herself because this must be bringing up
something in her past, obviously this is triggering something in her past."

Leopoldina: "Right, and that's bullshit. It's pure bullshit. And her present
is not totally fucked up with what's going on in there?"

Vin: "Being as angry as she is about her current situation. Being a capable
person, not being able to find a job that gives her any satisfaction. How is she
not going to be angry about not having a place to live for years on end and
now being treated like this, the way she's pathologized, the way other professionals look at her? All of this stuff. But, then Elizabeth and Hannah say that
it must be something in her past that led her to this place because if she wasn't
mentally ill, she wouldn't be there."

Leopoldina: "It's bullshit."

Vin: "Why would she be there? If you're a "normal" person, you wouldn't
be homeless. That's the whole underlying assumption that we work on."

Leopoldina: "It's not normal. It may be the norm, but it's not right. I don't
know how anyone can know Ariel for any amount of time and not see her
brilliance and the truth in the things she says."

Vin: "But, it comes up so much with staff at the shelter. Even during the interviews for the rooming house, it came up again. Donna was saying that she wasn't safe."

Leopoldina: "The tea, the fucking tea water."

Vin: "Right, she's going to burn down the house."

Leopoldina: "And then I would say how come it never happens on my shift? How come? How come she never burns the house down on my shift?"

Vin: "She's never burned the house or started a fire on any shift. But why did Donna bring that up again? Hannah said that Donna was really arguing against Ariel being in the house. She really thinks that she's mentally ill and not safe. I think that maybe she reacts that way to Ariel because she won't let her try to 'fix' her and then she doesn't know what else to do. If the problem is not with Ariel, it's too much to handle at the shelter."

Leopoldina and I both spoke with Ariel after that event and assured her that we agreed with her, but that maybe she could have not yelled at Hannah quite so much. We tried to openly explain why we thought Hannah reacted the way she did. Ariel agreed with our analysis: "I've known for awhile now that Hannah thinks of us as different. She won't admit it, but deep down she really thinks that she is better than us and is such a good person for helping us. We're not equals. If she valued me, she wouldn't treat me with such disrespect." Ariel felt reassured that Leopoldina and I supported her views, if not the timing and method of her virulent complaint: "It means a lot to have people who I can count on and who respect me instead of always trying to bring me down." We agreed that the best thing to do was to stay there and keep looking for a better place to stay.

During July 1996, Ariel finally came up on Amherst's waiting list for Section 8 housing. When Elizabeth and I talked with her, Ariel said she was willing to find an apartment and accepted the Section 8 subsidy. This was a change from the past. She used to be very reluctant to accept assistance because she felt she was capable of taking care of herself. I told her, "You have to think of it in terms of deserving. You are a good person. You don't do anything to harm anyone else. Don't you think you deserve, at the very least, a safe place to live?"

Ariel responded, "When I was homeless and living outside and having to try to sleep in the library or staying up all night in Stop and Shop, I didn't feel I deserved anything or had the right to be anywhere. I didn't have any right. Everywhere I went belonged to someone else and they were just letting me stay there for a little while. Even the shelter, I never had the right to stay there. You and Donna make Grove Street into a home, but it's still not my right to stay there. It's more that you are letting me. Living like that for years makes you think that you don't deserve a place of your own."

Vin, "You're right. It wasn't your right to stay at the shelter. If it was, they couldn't have made you go that summer when I was away for my honeymoon. I can see what you mean."

Ariel, "That's why I was ready to leave on my own this time. I didn't want the emotional suffering of being asked to leave the homeless shelter again."

A few weeks later I gave Ariel a ride downtown on a Wednesday afternoon. In the car, she discussed her frustration over not being able to find work: "I don't want people thinking that I don't want to work. I'm trying all I can. I send out résumés, call for every job I see in the paper, fill out applications, and never get a call back. I do a good job of cleaning too. Some of these places pay people good money and the place still is filthy after they're done. I explain how I could do a much better job and they just say, 'We're all set right now.' I can't just get a job. I don't have any control over getting a job. Somebody has to give me the job. It's so frustrating. I want to work. I need to work to pay for little things like food and some stockings every now and then, but nobody will give me a job. I don't know what else to do."

Finally, in December 1996, after almost five years of homelessness, Ariel found an apartment in Amherst which she could pay for with her housing subsidy. For the moment, she was housed due to her sheer ability to wait several years for her name to come up on the waiting list. Still without adequate income or employment and worrying about proposed cuts in food stamps and the possibility of further cuts in HUD and Section 8 certificates, Ariel could not feel very secure in her new home.

Within the homelessness industry, there is always an individual aberration that can be reformed or cared for. Once constructed, the categories such as mentally ill, victim of the foster-care system, substance abuser, and veteran become essentialized as the determinants of individual homelessness and indicators of pathology. Practices within the shelter focus on diagnosing, treating, retraining, and normalizing such deviancy. Homelessness and the homeless subject are produced in such a way as to support caring for and reforming deviant individual subjects at the exclusion of other possible efforts.

Everyone involved in this relationship did the best that they could given their understood "choices," but what was "possible" was constrained by both material and discursive conditions that remain largely unchallenged. Clearly, they are responding to their homelessness, but equally clear is how constrained those choices remain. Ariel's choices were limited to remaining homeless and searching for the right work, resisting the sheltering industry's medicalization of her homelessness and suffering the consequences that go with being non-compliant, giving up and declaring herself mentally disabled and possibly being allowed to live in a rooming house in poverty, or jumping off a bridge. The "choices" that homeless advocates and staff make are similarly discursively constrained. The normal, routine practices within the shelter silence anything but individual reform of "deviant others" or "helping" connect people with inadequate social services and virtually non-existent employment and housing opportunities.

CHAPTER 5

Defining the Role of the Sheltering Industry

VIN: *"Do you feel that you address any of the root causes of homelessness in your work?*

GLORIA: *"Most of the time, no, I don't. I think we have discussions about it, but I don't think that the way the work is set up is designed to do that.*

VIN: *"What prevents you from doing that?"*

GLORIA: *"Well, because the expectation is that I'm an expert and I'm going to help you. You're coming to me because you need help. I will ask you questions about your problems. I will tell you how to solve your problems. I'm not paid to sit there and say don't you think it's unjust that you don't have a place to live and what can we do about that. I do that now, Leopoldina does that, you do that, but the way the job is set up, in order to do that you have to go around the basic parameters of your basic job description."*

The previous chapters focused on how helping practices within shelters serve to produce homeless subjects. But what about the people working at the shelter? I've worked in homeless shelters for over nine years. In my experience, the people working in shelters are often very committed to ending homelessness and are mostly quite caring and dedicated. They want to help homeless people and sincerely believe that, given available options, they are doing so.

However, as I explore in this chapter, their helping efforts often take a particular form of governmental intervention designed to reform poor people. Shelter staff are part of a longer history of experts and professional reformers who have played a key role in liberal efforts to resolve social problems through governing social relations. What I'm referring to here as governmental interventions are "the deliberations, strategies, tactics, and devices employed by authorities for making up and acting upon a population and its constituents to ensure good and avert ill" (Rose 1996a: 322).

Social workers, urban planners, public health officials, demographers, sociologists, and epidemiologists were developed to implement these governmental interventions during the last century. However, the liberal welfare state has recently been under attack. Both neoliberal and conservative policy makers have focused on dismantling state-run social programs in favor of privatized, market-based efforts. How has this recent growth of neoliberalism affected governmental interventions? Drawing on Nikolas Rose's work, I argue that government of the poor is not being eliminated but, rather, is just being done in new ways.

Whereas much attention was previously focused on providing some degree of social welfare and to govern a national society through public social services, the new focus is on individualized, market-based efforts and private non-profit organizations competing for government grants. People are being governed through such concepts as being a "responsible" community or family member (Rose 1996c). Rose argues that people are now governed through their commitments to particular communities of morality and identity. Being a member of a community entails a particular way of being a person. Rather than being governed by others, people are now encouraged to govern themselves as "responsible" or "contributing" community members if they wish to receive any material and social benefits. Most importantly, there is no guarantee of any degree of social welfare or social well-being for those failing in their responsibility as community members.

A new way of dividing people into deserving and undeserving has developed as people are divided into the affiliated and the marginalized. The marginalized are understood to be that way for one of two reasons: by their inability to properly govern themselves or manage themselves as subjects, or by their affiliation to "some kind of 'anti-community' whose morality, lifestyle or component is considered a threat or reproach to public contentment and political order" (Rose 1996c: 340). These people can only access previously "social" benefits through their ability to function in a competitive market. This is where the new role for the professional social reformers comes into play. They are trained to help people "help themselves" through becoming "self-responsible" community members.

The particular form of "the social" necessitates the creation of jobs for experts at governing through treating perceived pathology. It is no longer seen as possible to manage poor people with generic social workers. Rather, those understood as unable to care for themselves for one reason or another are now widely treated and managed by specialized experts. These professionals work to impart skills at self-management through therapy of the individual self, but also through the increasingly specialized aspects of "training." The focus on "training" for self-responsibility as a member of a community has not supplanted, but rather works as one aspect of, the previously described medicalization of homelessness. Just as Elliot Liebow found that the staff working at the shelter where he did research professed to be experts at helping homeless women (1993), the staff I worked with possessed a range of "expertise" in helping homeless people.

I am not arguing that staff members working in shelters are hired and trained with the intention to dominate or control homeless people by simply managing homelessness. Nor am I arguing that staff are fooled by the ideology of deviance to think that the problem lies only within homeless people. Rather, when a hypothesis of deviancy dominates the shelter, when self-help understandings dominate throughout the society, when all sorts of social problems are medicalized, and when "common sense" images of the homeless subject as deviant prevail, the dominant imaginings about homelessness create a framework of deviancy within which their practices are enmeshed.

The next three chapters explore this process of well-meaning staff struggling with trying to "help" homeless people. I look at how staff and administrators develop job descriptions, conduct hirings, and train staff. My analysis demonstrates how the practices of staff members who govern "the homeless" through managing and treating perceived deviancy are partially constrained by the conceptual frameworks and social milieu in which they function as well as the ways in which funding concerns govern how shelters operate. These governing practices establish a dichotomous relationship between the staff and homeless people.

The Need for Professional Staff

A significant change in the sheltering industry occurred during the 1990s. While homeless shelters were once thought of as filling a temporary, emergency housing need, the entire industry has taken on a much more specialized, transitional focus in recent years. As the homeless sheltering industry has grown and become established, more refined diagnostic tools, statistical record keeping, and categories of pathology have produced more complex typologies of homeless people.

Once, prototypical images of "the homeless" as alcoholic men and the deinstitutionalized mentally ill guided social-policy responses to homelessness. Now, the medicalized social pathologies and lack of skills widely understood as resulting in homelessness are much more defined. "The homeless" are routinely broken down into many categories of individual disorders necessitating specialized "experts" whose job it is to retrain and treat these aberrant subjects. Staff are hired and trained as experts focusing their reformative efforts on the "special issues" of veterans, drug abusers, homeless teens, homeless women, the elderly, the mentally ill, victims of a variety of post-traumatic stress, those leaving domestic violence, homeless families, the undereducated, and those in need of job training. When I first started working in homeless shelters during the mid 1980s, the only skills that were really necessary were empathy for homeless people, some knowledge of available social-service options, and the ability to manage often hectic situations. Most people were hired as general counselors or managers. Today, staff positions include substance abuse counselor, job trainer, life skills experts, experts at helping survivors of traumatic stress, and other, similar roles.

As experts, the staff are expected to conduct themselves in particular ways. For example, a staff conduct policy implemented in the shelter where I worked as well as three other area shelters in the mid 1990s mandated a therapeutic relationship with guests. The document elucidated a view that homeless people are ill and deviant. The policy legislates against any physical contact between staff and shelter guests except for a handshake. Becoming friends with homeless people or giving out one's home phone number was banned. Furthermore, it stated that staff should not have any discussions with homeless people about any political or personal beliefs. Likewise, social contact with any current or former guests of the shelter was prohibited. One shelter director even suggested that staff members should not even acknowledge a homeless person (even a formerly homeless person) whom they ran into on the street. Of course, grassroots organizing within or outside the shelters or engaging with homeless people in any sort of reflective examination of alternatives to self-blame is not possible within the parameters of this policy.

Despite most staff at the shelters agreeing with the behaviors mandated by this policy, a few staff disagreed. Gloria, for example, argued, "I find the document morally reprehensible. I find it offensive. I agree with one of my co-workers that it should be ripped in half and thrown in the garbage. I think it's really to keep up walls between staff and guests. The whole policy sets up people who are homeless as different than the people who are working there." What was especially troubling to some of the staff at the shelter was that the policy contradicted new practices that had just recently emerged at the shelter.

Rethinking Routine Practices

As many of us working in the shelter began to know people such as Ariel, Anthony, Howard, Maria, and Jenny over a period of years, it became much more difficult to continue operating as though their homelessness was caused by something wrong with them. A frustration at our inability to help end their homelessness set in. We saw ourselves presented with two options: either we could further reinforce uncritical beliefs that we simply needed more training in how to "help," or we could begin to rethink our assumed staff practices and treatment efforts. Many staff "chose" the first option. Over time, however, some shelter staff began to question these practices. As I began to analyze the effects of our practices, I began to understand our maintaining the role of "normalizing" perceived deviance as preventing us from considering alternative possibilities. The situation with Ariel served as a catalyst for me to begin rethinking practices.

I began to consider that, if our practices and actions were constrained by our understandings about what caused homelessness and what we should be doing, knowledge of new concepts and understandings might make new kinds of actions possible. In thinking in this way, I was self-consciously aware of the problematic position facing ethnographers as described by Ann and Leopoldina. Was I trying to "write a paper or get some real work done?" If I tried to intervene and change the practices, was I stepping outside of my role as an ethnographer? I decided that, while I did not have adequate answers about what we should be doing instead, I also realized that I had could not keep myself from engaging people in a critique of our practices when I saw people being harmed by those very practices.

I began to write and talk with guests, staff, and volunteers about the problematic effects and limitations of our efforts. Academic papers focusing on my analysis of the limitations of such practices were shared with shelter staff, guests, and administrators. I began to focus my energies in engaging in dialogues about shelter practices. While sometimes personalizing the critiques, Leopoldina, Gloria, and Ann eventually responded very enthusiastically to the idea of thinking about our work in new ways. Donna and Hannah were open to creating opportunities for staff to discuss how to do our work in better ways.

Significant staff changes also occurred at this time leading to Donna becoming director of the shelter, me becoming assistant director, and Leopoldina being hired as a case manager. Leopoldina brought to her work a personal history of being treated in a disparaging fashion by "helping" professionals working at the welfare department despite her graduate-school education. Donna and I brought a desire for a non-hierarchical, cooperative management structure to our new positions.

All of these factors converged into significant structural changes in the shelter. Donna was committed to exploring new ways in which staff and guests could work on homelessness. During the spring of 1995, we began to devote a half hour of each week's meeting to thinking about what we hoped to accomplish and what was preventing us from doing so. In an effort to begin breaking down hierarchies, the staff worked toward management by formal consensus. Bi-weekly house meetings were instituted where all staff and guests came together to discuss policies. Monthly potluck suppers were organized where ex-guests, staff, community members, administrators, and advisory board members were welcomed for an evening of informal community building.

In December 1995, organizational meetings began to be held on a weekly basis at the shelter. A faculty member from Smith College was hired to facilitate these meetings. Organizing the meeting on principles from Paulo Freire's work, he strove to create a forum where participants could learn from each other how to think and act in new ways. One of the first topics to come up at these meetings was a desire to discover how we could break down the defined dichotomy between staff and homeless people legislated by the staff conduct policy. We also began to work together on coming to new understandings about what was causing homelessness and challenging perceived root causes of homelessness. Wide-ranging and thoughtful discussions took place both on the connection between structural conditions and the growth of homelessness and about our practices within the shelter. Staff training, the staff conduct policy, shelter rules, case management, the need for community organizing, and activism around wages and housing were all topics of much debate at these meetings.

As the focus on reforming and monitoring guests was problematized over this period, staff members responded in a variety of ways. The following discussion is indicative of staff meetings throughout this period.

Gloria facilitated a discussion during one staff meeting of ideas discussed in Herbert Gans's book *The War Against the Poor* (1995). She described Gans's analysis of the demonizing of poor people throughout American history and how society gains a benefit from having a permanent underclass. We agreed that much the same was currently happening in terms of welfare reform, homelessness policies, and the judicial system. Gloria then stated how she now felt that many of our everyday staff practices were based upon this historical pathologizing of poor people and served to silence the possibility of our working against the systemic processes creating poverty and homelessness.

Gloria asked: "If we were willing to really attack the systemic causes of poverty and injustice, what risks would we be willing to take? And, starting with the premise that the problem is not the individual, but the societal structure may well be what is causing the underclass to exist. What I'd like to try to do is to try to identify five concrete status quo disruptors, five things that would really challenge the system. And, then narrow it down to one that we as staff could all agree on and try to take action on."

All the staff agreed that we were no longer satisfied with simply providing emergency shelter, but disagreements regarding what else we should do erupted. A long discussion followed where the staff debated a variety of strategies. Donna, for example, wanted the staff to focus on improving the efficacy of our case-management practices within the shelter and develop more effective job training in the shelter so that we could "help" more homeless people. She asked, "Can we develop an in-house education program and an entrepreneurial venture … so that people could both earn a living wage and also get education and skills…. And also to bring in additional revenue for the shelter."

I pointed out how homelessness grew during a period of wealth being transferred toward the richest people in the country and suggested that what was needed to end homelessness was political action aimed at decreasing systemic inequality. I suggested that we try to work in coalitions with homeless people, labor and social-justice groups to do something about the wages paid in local jobs. Several staff members (Gloria, Ann, and Leopoldina in particular) were enthused by the prospects of doing something about wages.

I then restated Gloria's question about risk taking: "Now, to go along with the question about risk taking, if we work with people to try to organize a union at a local business in town or we organize a consumer boycott or we try to have a meal tax to try to support affordable housing or if we try to do any of these things, I wonder how that's going to affect rich people in town wanting to donate money to us." All of the staff agreed that was a concern, but no one had a solution.

We then discussed the possibilities of social actions to address wages. Most staff agreed that we could not expect non-unionized workers at local restaurants or retail stores to take a lead role in such efforts. The risks of being punished by the employer for such actions were seen as too great. In fact, a local worker who had tried to organize downtown restaurant workers in Northampton a few years previously informed the shelter staff of several instances of employer retaliation against workers involved in that effort.

Robert replied: "If the public was really aware, that couldn't happen. They can only get away with that in a climate that would believe all of these things happening and leave them unexamined. We talk about solving homelessness, but one of the ways it can happen is to get the community involved in understanding all of the different ways that impact people and homelessness is just one of them."

Leopoldina: "That's what I've been thinking. I was thinking that we could do more outreach and learn to speak in front of people. If we made an effort to write more letters and to do public speaking. All of us. And to bring the causes of homelessness together for people. I don't mean in an orthodox, typical education. And that means elementary schools and right up. How can you exploit another human being? How do you go to bed at night and have a vacation and a second home? How the hell do you live with yourself?"

All staff articulated a view that they would rather spend more time working toward decreasing what they understood as the root political-economic causes of homelessness. The dominant view, however, remained that "we have to focus on what we can do" or "we have to do something to help the actual people we work with to give them tools to cope with the reality they live under." Many staff members believed that they were powerless to change any aspect of social inequality. Additionally, staff, including myself, had a quite difficult time envisioning new practices that did not emphasize changing the individual. Most ideas about new practices coming out of these discussions simply switched from an emphasis on treating medical disorders within home-less people toward developing practices better able to help homeless people become employed through training.

Despite the newly developed awareness, it was still rare for staff to resist their role as "helping" professionals. An overwhelming amount of staff time continued to be spent in surveillance, monitoring, and reforming of home-less people. As we began to problematize our practices, many of the staff became increasingly frustrated with our inability to do more "substantive" work. Analyzing how the shelter staff attempted to do "more substantive" work through examining the hiring of new staff, responding to an increasing number of young homeless people, and altering shelter polices and rules dem-onstrates how the actual daily practices sustained the relationship of "help-ing" staff members and homeless people as clients with disorders needing to be fixed. What changed were simply the methods by which these "helping" practices were accomplished.

Treating Deviancy or Organizing for Social Change: A Contentious Staff Hiring

At a shelter meeting in May 1995, the discussion moved from complaining about the way homeless people were represented in a HUD grant application to a discussion of how staff members would like to work. Our constant fis-cal battle for survival and the lack of money to hire adequate staffing were often cited as reasons why we could not do "more substantive work" at the shelter. "More substantive work" was largely Donna's euphemism for work more effective in treating disorders within homeless selves, but Ann, Gloria, Leopoldina, and I disagreed. We envisioned a variety of staff practices aimed at addressing issues including jobs for homeless people, job training, commu-nity organizing around the need for more shelters, and efforts to educate the local public about the political-economic components of homelessness.

Donna would often justify prevailing practices by saying, "Everyone is just flat out and can't do any more. The problem is our bare-bones staffing." I heard over and over again from service providers, staff, and advocates that "we know what works, we just need more money to provide more services." The grant application was presented as a potential way of providing the fund-ing needed for increased staffing to enable us to do the work we envisioned.

A controversy arose, however, over the question of what those new staff members would do. Several staff and administrators envisioned more funding as providing an opportunity to hire more staff with skills in case management for mentally ill homeless people, substance-abuse treatment, and job training. The grant application to HUD was written with those goals in mind.

Ann: "The grant is written in such a way that we'll end up with case managers and social workers. Is that what we want to do? What about advocacy or organizing?"

Vin: "That's no surprise to me. We don't do organizing or educational stuff. If we got more people to work here, what would they do? With the people we have here now, what should we do?"

Robert: "Agitate and organize. Go out to the post office. Really. Be gadflies. Get out there and really shake it up. Make this a real public debate and have the time to do it. I just don't have the time with my two jobs. That's one idea."

Vin: "So, if you have an outreach worker. Maybe outreach not to other homeless people, but to…."

Robert: "Yeah, absolutely. The problem is not individually oriented to 'homeless people,' but it's about the context that they exist within. Have someone who regularly goes to the town government meetings and talks about the issues that regularly come up … around who can afford to live in this town. If you really bump it up, that will become a focus for everybody."

Vin: "So, is there any way for us to think about doing something like that with our hours and our staffing? It seems like lots of us try to do some of that in our non-work, extra time, but is there a way to make it part of our jobs?"

Robert: "It's hard to make a regular commitment when it's not [a part of the staff job description]. When you start to have 3:00 in the morning meetings, I could do it. When everyone's asleep, I could agitate." [Robert worked two other jobs in addition to his job at the shelter. The only free hours in his day were between midnight and 7 am].

Leopoldina: "But, I think that the problem is our job descriptions and duties. When I was hired, for example, it was as a case manager. They said, 'now you're not going to like this, we're going to call it a case manager and we know you're not going to like it, but we have to.' And, these new staff, if we got this grant, would be coming in to do case management also. Case management is what takes up our time."

Ann: "Here's the other thing. I'm supposed to be writing some kind of a grant to replace my position [she was employed in the shelter as a Vista worker] and I've been avoiding it for three months because I don't want to replace my position. I'm thinking that this is giving me food for thought. I can write a grant saying that we want someone to come in to do political education, we want someone to go out and do political education. We want somebody to stir things up. It could be in some ways an organizing and educational position."

Robert: "What we would be doing is setting up something where someone could establish a relationship with people outside of the shelter. That's what I'm hoping."

Unfortunately, Robert's hope did not materialize. The shelter did not receive the grant from HUD. However, in February 1996, we received a significant amount of state funding that created the opportunity to hire two additional staff members. Job descriptions were written by Donna or Hannah. One position was to work during the day with primary emphasis on case management of younger homeless people and creating workshops and job trainings for guests in the shelter. The second job would be mostly an evening position of "site manager" with additional case management and surveillance duties at the shelter. All staff and administrators had agreed that organizing for social change with both guests and housed community members was a necessary part of all of our work, but these job descriptions failed to address that task. Instead, the qualification listed in the job posting included "experienced with the homeless population and knowledge of alcoholism and addiction issues and recovery. Bi-lingual (Spanish) preferred. Must have reliable transportation. Excellent organizational skills required." What was not included was any knowledge or understanding of class inequality, exploitative local labor conditions under which 40 per cent of our guests worked, or a knowledge of community organizing.

I brought this omission to the attention of other staff and shelter guests. I asked them what qualities were omitted from the advertisement. There was very little public response to my question. In private, though, Gloria, Ann, and Leopoldina each argued that the advertisement was evidence that those running the shelter still understood that homelessness was caused by shortcomings within homeless people. As Gloria, who was applying for one position, said, "Well, whoever wrote that is using the model that the people are broken and need to be fixed. So, in a sense it's saying that you're really dealing with disease here, you're dealing with something that needs to be challenged in a certain direction."

Vin: "So, why do you think that happened?"

Gloria: "Well, I guess it goes back to that some people really believe that homelessness is really the fault of the individual person as opposed to seeing it as a systemic issue. So, the response to homelessness is to try to cure the person and reintegrate the person into society at large."

Vin: "Why do you think that knowledge and experience with community organizing or economic inequality were not listed as necessary qualifications?

Gloria: "Because, I don't think that the agencies want to do that. I don't think that they're interested in challenging society. I don't think that they're interested in organizing a movement of people who are angry or dispossessed."

After another contentious debate, hiring committees were established consisting of shelter administrators, Donna, and different staff members for each position. Over 40 applicants sent résumés and cover letters detailing their training and qualifications for working in a shelter. Most often, applicants discussed their social-work training, knowledge of self-help programs, experience with mental-health or substance-abuse counseling, or personal experiences with substance abuse as evidence of their ability to work as a shelter staff members.

Another antagonistic series of encounters preceded each hiring committee's finalizing their interview questions. I, along with a few other staff members, wanted questions about how applicants understood homelessness. While placating my wishes with one question—"What factors do you think have led to the recent increased numbers of homeless people and how should we respond to that?"—most interview questions focused on the ability of the potential staff to govern homeless people. Another question asked, "As an emergency shelter, guests are allowed to stay for 60 days per year. Extensions are granted on a case-by-case basis. Approximately 25 per cent return the following year needing shelter. What do you think would be the most appropriate staff response to this phenomenon?" I was hoping that even one applicant would state that the most appropriate response would be for staff to work with guests and other community members to create more shelter space and affordable housing. That did not happen. Instead, applicants stressed that we needed to figure out how to work more effectively to treat and train guests while they were at the shelter so that fewer people needed to return. One applicant suggested that she would "help individuals identify the traits they need to work on to prevent a recurrence of homelessness." Additional questions asked about applicants' experience with substance-abuse and mental-health counseling, what types of workshops they might develop in the shelter to train homeless people, how they would fairly enforce shelter rules, what the unique needs of homeless teens might be, and how they would approach a combative and drunk homeless guest.

Both the listed skills of applicants and the questions chosen indicate that the most important role of a shelter staff member remained governing homeless people. Gloria, although she had the most experience, was not hired for either position. She and I both believe that she was not hired because of her outspoken unwillingness to define her role to only that of governing homeless people.

Two other applicants were eventually hired. As Donna and Hannah strongly emphasized a need for someone with "knowledge of substance abuse issues," one new staff member, Aaron, was hired in large part because of his self-professed "recovery" from a drug-abusing past. It was understood that his experiences would enable him, a white man in his late 20s, to better detect and treat drug users. Aaron was hired to manage the physical household, increase staff expertise at treating substance use, and provide further counseling skills.

A second person, Karen, was hired primarily because of her professed expertise at treating homeless youth. Karen, a white woman in her early 20s, was responsible for developing workshops for guests, developing a special program for younger guests, and assisting with case management. When I asked Karen and Donna what type of workshops were envisioned, their responses included budgeting skills, résumé writing, stress management, interview skills, how to search for housing, and possible AA/NA meetings in the shelter. Organizing these workshops became a primary focus of her job. During the first six months of working in the shelter, Karen organized a variety of workshops on money management, housing searches, nutrition, creative writing, substance abuse, anger management, and smoking cessation. None mentioned the collective or socio-economic experience of homelessness.

A few months later, Karen expressed frustration at her job. She said that she felt that no one in the shelter liked her because she could not develop "real relationships" with them because she couldn't "act naturally." She described how she believed she had to act "like some little social worker who knows what's best for everyone." I asked Karen if her training had included anything about working collectively with shelter guests or doing any community organizing. Karen replied, "Organizing? I was kind of discouraged from it.... What do you mean by organizing? ... I was discouraged from doing any of that by Donna and Rachel."

After two years of discussions among shelter staff examining staff practices and questioning our mission at the shelter, we now had hired additional staff. Some of us hoped that this new funding would provide an opportunity to organize and form ties with social justice organizations. Others hoped we could do community organizing. Yet, when we did hire new staff, the director and administrators discouraged them from doing that work.

Staff Policing as Detection and Training

As we began to rethink our jobs and interactions with homeless people at the staff meetings and shelter-wide "organizing" meetings, the assumptions behind some rules began to be questioned. One immediate modification in practices was an increased awareness of the effect of shelter rules on defining the relationship between the staff and homeless guests. As a consequence, staff and guests began to examine shelter rules in an effort to make them more effective, to use them in ways that are "really working with the guests instead of pathologizing them." By this, however, some staff simply meant that they wanted to revise the rules so as to move away from staff punishing homeless people and toward staff policing of the guests as a more refined method of treating deviancy. As the following two examples demonstrate, the primary defined relationship remained one where staff maintained the role of "normalizing" homeless individuals through detecting and treating (through discipline) disorders within homeless people. The only real change was the means by which the governing occurred.

Prior to this period of staff reflection about the efficacy of the policies and rules, staff policing of guests was conceptualized as functioning to train homeless people through punishing them. For example, it was understood that a staff member making a homeless person who had returned to the shelter after curfew spend the night outside was a tool for teaching that homeless person the self-discipline and self-responsibility needed to be a successful employee in future jobs. The new problematization of shelter policies simply resulted in changing staff practices from training through punishment to training through rewarding the efforts of homeless people to be responsible community members.

In the effort to restructure shelter operations, rules clearly based on punishing guests were called into question. Staff began to spend time seeking alternative strategies to help guests to work more effectively on "their issues." As a result, several rules were altered, yet the construction of staff as "helping" professionals remained.

TRAINING THROUGH REWARDS

Shelter staff had long maintained a 10:30 curfew. If guests did not have permission to be out later, they would lose their bed. Employment was the only acceptable reason for being late in most cases. This curfew was applied so strictly that many homeless people were routinely prevented from visiting their families at Christmas, attending sober dances on New Years Eve, or simply seeing a movie downtown. It was argued that staff would be unable to help homeless people if they were not in the shelter and they needed to be in at a "reasonable" hour if they wanted to demonstrate responsibility for working on "their issues."

Most people at the shelter willingly complied with this policy while stating they were grateful to be able to stay out even that late. A few other people (usually younger guests) attempted to get around the rule by making up stories to explain why they were late getting back to the shelter and pledging to be "more responsible" in the future. Sometimes this tactic aroused staff sympathy, but sometimes they lost their place and had to sleep outdoors. However, the fact that very few guests ever articulated a desire to change the shelter curfew policy does not mean that most agreed with it. Many people disagreed with the rule but silenced their displeasure as they felt powerless to change it. They realized that curfews were routine at virtually every shelter, functioning as a means for staff to govern the people living at the shelter. Guests felt that staff would not change the rule because that would decrease their power to monitor homeless people. Many different homeless people expressed such a sentiment to me, but only when I mentioned I had problems with the rule.

When staff began to consider training homeless people through "offering carrots," extending the curfew and allowing nights out were quickly raised as the most obvious benefits to offer in exchange for more cooperation with case-management mandates. We discussed possible incentives that could be put in place at the shelter to reward compliant guests. A new policy was put into place allowing a guest to stay out until midnight in return for a week's worth of chores in the house. Guests could take a night out of the shelter if they did two weeks of daily chores.

The decision to implement this policy of responsible work in exchange for increased liberty was a difficult one. This discussion began when I asked in a staff meeting, "Instead of all of our work [being] focused on punishment, maybe positive incentives would help. A lot of the trouble that younger people who stay here have historically gotten into with staff have been in terms of coming back by 10:30. All they want is to stay out a little later with some friends. They tell us some story and we get into this dynamic of them lying and us getting mad for their not 'being responsible.' But why do they need to be in by 10:30 every night?"

Gloria, Donna, and Karen initially argued that we would only be courting trouble if we moved in such a direction. They assumed that guests would most likely be using drugs or alcohol if they were out later. As Karen explained, "I'm not so sure of how to do it. I don't have much experience with using carrots instead of sticks. I've always been uncomfortable with curfews on adults, but one reason is that if you have a job, you shouldn't be out all night. Or, if you're out at night, you'll probably be using [drugs or alcohol]." Gloria voiced a similar opinion at that meeting. Interestingly, neither one of them saw the irony when I mentioned that they had jobs and were often out past 10:30.

Eventually, we decided to experiment with an extended curfew on an interim basis. The main selling point for staff was that it was an alternative strategy to help staff to train guests to become more responsible and self-disciplined, to govern them in new ways. Much the same occurred with a second shelter policy; the rule about the use of drugs and alcohol.

RETHINKING SELF-HELP

As was explained earlier, shelter staff strictly banned any use by guests of alcohol or illegal drugs while staying at the shelter. If staff surveillance detected the use of alcohol or drugs, a written warning would be issued. A second written warning meant that the guest would be banned from the shelter for at least 30 days. To get back into the shelter, the homeless person needed to go through an appeal process. At this hearing, the guest would discuss what had changed in his or her life to indicate a readiness to follow the rules. Most often this entailed promises of attending a 12-step program and entering a drug treatment program.

This policy was the center of much discussion and debate over the years. The original rationale for having the rule was the assumption that many people were homeless due to substance-abuse problems and, to help them help themselves, we needed to break down their "denial" and force them to "work their 12-step program." A related reason was the view that many of the guests at the shelter were in early "recovery" and, to make the house "safe" for them, we needed to ensure that people would not return smelling of alcohol. As a result of this rule, over 80 people were given warnings during 1992 and 1993 and several guests were banned from the shelter. When asked, most guests voiced their support for the policy because they also believed that the way to resolve homelessness was through their learning to treat substance abuse through self-reform.

Leopoldina and I questioned if we were really helping people by denying them shelter because they had fallen short of our case-management demands; we wondered why we didn't base the rule on behavior. I asked the other staff, "Doesn't everyone deserve a place to sleep which is safe and warm?" We argued that staff were perpetuating the division of "the homeless" into deserving and undeserving by denying shelter to those whom we deemed to be undeserving based on an inability or unwillingness to comply with our "helping" rules. Most other staff, on the other hand, expressed more concern with developing a fair way of enforcing the rule. Donna, Gloria, and Ann all accepted that the best way for staff to help homeless people involved teaching homeless people to govern themselves through, for example, not using drugs and alcohol. Their only voiced concern was over how we were able to discern the use of drugs. Donna and Karen suggested drug testing. This "solution" was raised at three different times in two years, but the staff sentiment was overwhelmingly against it.

Several meetings involving guests and staff at the shelter took place during the fall of 1995 in an effort to re-examine the policy. A variety of issues were raised. For instance, I raised a concern with having a rule that is impossible to really enforce because of the difficulty of detecting drugs and alcohol use. Donna was concerned about safety and the potential for increased violence if people under the influence of drugs or alcohol stayed in the shelter. Her solution to the inability to detect drug use was to allow for random drug testing of guests suspected of using drugs. She also expressed the need for staff to provide better education and support around recovery and addiction issues. Hannah, meanwhile, voiced concern about our different expectations for the housed and the homeless. She argued, "Don't the unhoused also have a right to drink without losing their housing?"

What eventually came out of the meeting was a suggestion to slightly alter our rule while maintaining the policing role of shelter staff. We compromised with an agreement not to have drug testing, but also not to allow anyone to return to the shelter after drinking. Instead, our revised policy was rationalized as an attempt to improve techniques of reforming deviancy. Instead of a second warning resulting in expulsion from the shelter, the suggestion was that homeless people would be given the opportunity to develop a contract for further stays at this point. This contract would stipulate how they were going to work with staff to address their "substance abuse problem." This was seen as a more effective way of training homeless people as they would necessarily be agreeing to take an active role in governing their own behavior. When this suggestion was brought up for discussion, the debate unfolded as follows.

Donna stressed that she felt we needed to be more effective in helping substance-abusing guests with their efforts at self-help. She suggested that staff needed to be more effective both in detecting drug use and in using the practice of giving warnings as an opportunity to develop contracts to engage guests in agreeing to treat their own substance abuse disorder: "My feeling is that we need to have at least one concrete and verifiable treatment option in each contract ... just to verify that they are, for example, attending therapy.... Or going to a drug treatment program...."

Gloria suggested that we should still mandate that any guest who returned to the shelter after using drugs or alcohol needed to stay out for a set period of time. She envisioned this as a means of teaching self-discipline through punishment. "What about the idea of a mandatory or minimum stay out?" Donna responded to that suggestion: "Either that or a set plan where you have to go through a long-term treatment like we did with Luke and we're trying to do with Jim. Because I wouldn't even want Jim to go out and sit in the woods drinking for thirty days and then come back. I want to make sure it's constructive and that the person has some firm commitment demonstrated before they come back."

Eventually, most staff agreed to alter the rule with the provision of a contract. Included within this contract was a stipulation that the homeless person would need to consent to increased monitoring of their daily activities by staff. For example, some contracts contained language whereby a guest would have to consent to allow staff to call substance-abuse counselors, therapists, or outpatient programs regarding their attendance at these treatment options. Others mandated a one-week stay at a drug treatment program or daily attendance at 12-step meetings. Most guests also appreciated this rule. Many stated that it showed that the staff were still really concerned with helping guests with the issues that made them homeless.

As with the curfew, staff clearly wanted to revamp shelter policies in ways that they perceived as being more beneficial. These well-meaning efforts resulted in altered policies. However, because the role of the shelter staff remained defined as governing homeless people, the altered rules simply involved changed methods of control and training. The underlying purpose of the shelter staff remained unchanged in terms of daily practices.

Despite the long discussions surrounding this effort to revise the policy, staff raised the issue of drug testing again at a staff meeting in May 1996. Donna wanted us to discuss her perception of heroin use in the house and how we were going to catch users. It all surrounded two guests whom some staff suspected of using heroin. They both came to the house from drug treatment programs with the intention of simply waiting for a space at a halfway-house program. These two men also stated that they were going to attend a local day-treatment program and go to 12-step meetings. Some of their behaviors and appearance, however, indicated heroin use as they would nod off during the day and sometimes scratch their arms.

Donna said, "The word on the street is that they are using daily." Rachel agreed with Donna by saying that people had also approached her about drug use at Grove Street. While two staff, Paul and Aaron, argued that it would be too expensive and time consuming to test and they weren't sure of the ethics of selective testing, Leopoldina and I adamantly opposed the proposal. Karen, who had always favored standardized drug testing as a diagnostic device, again argued for drug testing: "I can't do my job if they are using." Karen was right. She could not "do her job" most effectively without having drug testing available because of the way she understood her job. For Karen to effectively help homeless people govern themselves, they needed to cooperate with her and accept that she had the key to helping them.

Karen continued: "Most other shelters do it. I don't see what's wrong with it. If someone wants us to help them, they should be expected to stay clean. There are 50 people on our waiting list and the people at the cot program. Why don't we help those people who want help?" Again, Karen was suggesting that a proper role for the shelter staff was in determining who was deserving, or undeserving, of our "help." A homeless person must want the staff's help; otherwise, the homeless person is not working to become a responsible, community member and, therefore, do not deserve "help" or even deserve the former "social right" of a place to live. This is a clear example of what Nikolas Rose (1996c) refers to as the end of "social rights" under the dismantled welfare state. Even these self-proclaimed progressive staff members cannot see housing (even in a shelter) as a social right. Instead, people deserve the privilege of housing only if they are "self-responsible" community members in the competitive market for shelter beds.

Donna continued to argue for drug testing: "The behavior is disrupting the house. It makes it impossible for us to have a dry shelter without drug testing and more difficult for other guests to stay clean when some are using. How can we work with someone if they are using and won't be honest with us? It fosters lies around the house."

Vin: "What fosters the lies are rules that [say], if you are honest with us and tell us you are using, you will be asked to leave and will have to live on the street."

Leopoldina: "I see testing as a real violation. It's done because it's easy and simple and expedient. Those are all the wrong reasons. I also believe there is a difference between substance use and substance abuse." Most staff, however, refused to address this distinction between use and abuse.

Karen: "But, we're not helping anyone by just enabling them here."

Leopoldina: "How are we helping Mike and Mark [two ex-shelter guests who were kicked out of the shelter a number of times and were now living on the railroad tracks] by having kicked them out? They are living outside now and are just about ready to drink themselves to death. I just have a hard time with that tough love stuff."

Donna and Karen responded to Leopoldina's concern by arguing that most other homeless shelters in the area had routine drug testing. Similarly, Rachel suggested that, as we moved toward more of a "transitional" role as defined by HUD's "continuum of care" model, we needed to have drug testing as an option to be used to "help" guests. Although we avoided instituting drug testing at that time, policing homeless people is one "common sense" technique by which staff train them and thus manage homelessness.

CHAPTER 6

Helping Homeless Youth

Northampton, like many communities, saw an increasing number of homeless people in their late teens and early twenties throughout the 1990s. During the summer of 1995 the presence of several homeless young adults spending their days in a downtown city park received much local attention. Small crowds of homeless youth hanging out with housed teenagers playing hackeysack, skateboarding, sometimes drinking alcohol, having drum circles, and sometimes smoking and selling marijuana were soon portrayed as a major social problem in the press and in planning meetings involving local politicians and social-service providers. Attention from the police, local merchants, local political leaders, the press, and various social-service agencies began to focus on these young people as a social problem. Over the next several years, a variety of responses emerged. Several public meetings were held, funding was dedicated to new staff positions to help homeless youth, and, eventually, new laws were passed. The responses illustrate a desire to manage public homelessness so that young homeless people either became less visible or came to more fully embrace cultural whiteness.

The initial responses came from the shelter staff. Shelter staff compiled data documenting an over 50-per-cent increase in homeless youth. These data, along with human-interest stories about their lives, were then shared with the local press and used to apply for funding for new staff positions. Karen was hired to work with younger people. In addition, the city planning department helped obtain funding to hire an "outreach therapist" through the YWCA. This person tried to get to know homeless young people so that they would then comply with referrals to treatment and training programs.

Within the shelter, many of the younger guests were receiving warnings because of their unwillingness or inability to follow all the shelter policies and case-management guidelines, but most staff were unwilling to resort to the tried and failed method of simply kicking these youths out of the shelter. Staff, though, were becoming frustrated by their lack of options to help these guests. We would see many of the same people year after year and felt frustrated by our inability to help them. In response, shortly after being hired, Karen developed a "teen track."

The "teen track" consisted primarily of training to help staff help these young people. Based on compiled statistics about "typical" homeless teens, the plan was to develop profiles of young homeless people. Based on these profiles, staff were taught to look for symptoms of what shortcomings caused each particular person's homelessness and how to help treat them. Karen also developed a set of workshops on job training and tried to establish a mentoring program. Mentors would provide advice on work skills to the young people, but, unfortunately, very few mentors were ever located. Self-help programs for substance abuse would be nearly mandated, as would counseling sessions for those diagnosed as having mental-health issues.

I asked Hannah, who co-wrote the grant applications for Karen's position, what she envisioned being accomplished with the "teen track." Her reply made it clear that her emphasis was on training: "I conceived of it as a way of setting up trainings or groups that we could offer people to try to engage the young people to address the reality of where they are at … limit setting … [to teach them that] when somebody says no, that's the limit." Hannah's proposed solution to "teen homelessness" was for staff to function as parent figures enforcing strict limits and discipline on the younger homeless guests. Her assumption was that they were homeless because they lacked the skills needed to get a decent paying job and not because of the pay they received in the jobs where they were working, housing costs, or the unwillingness of a few of them to embrace habits and work lives that they found to be repulsive.

Despite the well-intentioned helping efforts of Hannah, Karen, and the outreach therapist, these efforts proved very ineffective in decreasing homelessness. A particular concern for many of the staff was that many of the young people were not cooperative with staff efforts and attendance at group meetings was sparse unless the meetings were made a condition of staying at the shelter.

An 18-year-old African-American woman, Susan, was at the shelter for several months. During her stay, she consistently maintained a job working in a fast-food restaurant. Her pay, however, was never going to be enough to pay her share of the expenses for an apartment in town. The staff didn't exactly know what to do to help Susan. However, through a series of case-management meetings, shelter staff diagnosed Susan as suffering the effects of emotional and sexual abuse from her youth and from a lack of job skills. Staff suggested therapy as a treatment for her PTSD and emotional issues, job training, and life-skills education. Finally, we referred her to a residency program for homeless teens where she could theoretically receive some job training. Susan did not like this option: "Why the fuck would I want to do that and live by their fucking rules? I was already in the Job Corps and I'm still homeless." Eventually, Susan became pregnant, moved to a family shelter, and became eligible for governmental assistance which enabled her to rent an apartment that she couldn't afford while she had been working.

Some people, like Susan, resisted (although not using that term) the language and practices through which staff and policy makers attempted to help them. Other young people living on the streets would not even come into the shelter or talk to the outreach worker because of shelter rules and what they perceived as efforts to "normalize" them. Often they felt a deep sense of alienation from, and disappointment in, the larger culture and did not want to be "fixed" or "normalized" to take part in what they saw as an exploitative society.

One young woman, Amy, described these efforts in a way that was representative of many other young people I spoke with about efforts to help them: "I don't know. It's hard living on the streets, but it's not too bad except when I'm given a hard time for panhandling. What's really hard is that everyone wants to change me and make me 'normal.' I don't want to be normal. I hate what that means. Why can't I just be me and still have a place to live and food to eat?"

The expressed sentiment among staff, shelter administrators, and policy makers regarding "difficult" homeless people like Amy was that there was little we could do to help her "type" because she was unwilling to help herself. An outreach worker, though, would attempt to work with such youths over a period of time to develop a trusting relationship in an effort to have them cooperate more with the available service providers. Such cooperation, however, would eventually entail exactly what Amy described as "trying to make me normal." The practices of this professional outreach worker aimed to incorporate homeless youth living on the streets into the regime of monitoring and treatment, making them into a compliant "case." Likewise, the focus of the public fora was always on how to provide the services needed to fix what was wrong with the young homeless people and on how to convince them to utilize available reformative services.

There are many alternative ways in which staff working in the sheltering industry could work with people like Amy and Susan who took oppositional stances toward "helping" efforts. Staff could work with Amy and her friends to try to develop strategies so that she could "be me" and still have a place to live and food to eat. This, however, would mean that they would be working together to create a society where housing was a "social right." Staff could understand the use of drugs, body piercing, and cooperative living on the streets of the city by some homeless youth as acts of resistance. With that type of understanding, staff might work together with homeless teens to create a less exploitative society from which they felt less alienated. They could do this, though, only if they had the conceptual framework for thinking in those terms and were willing to step outside of the hierarchical power relationships that they were expected to maintain.

Understandably, when standard treatment efforts proved largely ineffective, shelter staff and administrators were desperate for new and better ways to help these young people. As a result, in June 1996 the director of a nearby program for homeless young adults was invited to a shelter staff meeting at Karen's suggestion. The meeting began with the director of the program enumerating some of their programs and what they offered young people. He explained that, for everyone who comes to the program, they develop a plan of where they want to go and what resources there are to help them get there. The young person needs to be employed, give a percentage of their income to the program, save a percentage, and stick to the program. If they do not, they are kicked out of the program. When I then asked how he defined "success" and if he had percentages of people who stick with the program for over a year, or for three or four years, he said he didn't have that data because they did not collect it.

During this one-hour discussion, it became quite clear that Hannah, Rachel, Donna, Karen, and Robert understood that the way to help young homeless people was through the professional staff acting in a more authoritative manner in the shelter while holding young people more accountable for their personal homelessness. As Hannah stated, "we're not doing anybody any favors by being too liberal and not developing systems and structures to make them work on their problems." Karen agreed: "All I'm trying to do is figure out a way to do my job of helping the people staying here. I just think that if we can get them to develop a plan of where they want to go, work harder, and be more accountable for their actions then we'll be helping them more." Karen was defining her job as treating "the homeless" through coercion, discipline, and training. At this meeting, she was hoping to find tools to be more effective in accomplishing what she understood her job to be. Her desire to develop a clear treatment plan for each young homeless person was portrayed as a way of working more effectively.

Leopoldina, however, asked, "So, are they going to develop the plan or are we as staff going to develop the plan? What if someone decided that their goal for the next 60 days is to become the best badminton player possible? Will we support them in that decision or will we make a more 'realistic' plan for them?" Karen, Rachel, Hannah, and Robert said that of course we would tell them that they needed to make a more realistic plan. The ultimate authority to develop the treatment plan lay in the hands of the professional staff. The assumption was that they, the staff, were housed and therefore knew what was best for homeless people.

Aaron questioned this assumption, however. He pointed out that young homeless people often did not go to the workshops and training offered precisely because they did not see how the prescribed treatments would help them escape the dire poverty and homelessness. Many homeless people had been through workshops, treatment programs, and counseling time after time and they were still homeless. When I agreed with Aaron by suggesting that staff could instead work collectively with homeless people in organizing for political and economic change in the community, most staff dismissed that as "unrealistic" and not an acceptable use for the grant money.

As the following conversation with Karen indicates, many of the staff pushing for more effective staff practices for treating deviancy within homeless people philosophically agreed with our assessment that what was needed were more services and broader structural changes. However, they felt that they were powerless to bring about such systemic changes. In lieu of acting collectively and powerfully, these staff are inclined to concede that guests must learn to cope by fitting into society, even when the homeless person might want that least of all.

Karen explained: "See, honestly, I see the bigger spectrum, but then I also see someone who makes choices within where they are that might make things worse for themselves."

Vin: "But, are they really choices? Aren't the choices available awfully constrained?"

Karen: "I mean … maybe they're suffering also from the dynamics of the family they grew up in, which doesn't mean they deserve to be homeless or anything. Shouldn't we help them with that?"

I then questioned how much our efforts to treat understood pathologies within these young people were helping by discussing the staff treatment of Jacob. Jacob was one of the guests whom the "teen track" was specifically designed to help. He'd been a guest at the shelter several times over the past two years and many staff members were quite dismayed at their inability to "motivate" this intelligent young man to "get his life back on track." Several staff were arguing against letting him back into the shelter because he was uncooperative with our treatment plans. Jacob is not willing to work in what he sees as a completely corrupt system; he would rather live in shelters or outside. He's young, very intelligent, and very disgusted by the society he lives in. He works hard when he decides that a task is useful or necessary; he spent one entire summer taking care of younger homeless teens in the city, spending hours each day finding food and places for these people to sleep. Yet he is unwilling to get a haircut and to go to work each day at a food-service job.

In an effort to help Jacob, the staff attempted the same "tough love" treatment that they tried with Ariel. They gave him an option of cooperating with the treatment plan or living outside. The stated belief of Elizabeth, Donna, and Hannah was that "maybe he'll learn some responsibility and sense if he has to live outside." I suggested to Karen that what he'd learned is that the staff at the shelter are intent on "normalizing" him just like his parents were. I asked, "can't we work with him where he is and respect his ability to make decisions and reason and ask if there is anything we can work together on to make his decision to not be part of the system he holds in disdain any easier?" Karen's response was, "I don't know. I mean, if you're in this society, you have to learn to fit in. Otherwise, it's hard to figure out how to start. It's overwhelming to think of how you are going to make changes in this society."

Such a sentiment is hardly surprising. As Comaroff and Comaroff state, "Most people live in worlds in which many signs, and often the ones that count the most, look as though they are eternally fixed" (1991: 17). Where do you start? Both Leopoldina and Karen expressed their clear frustration at not knowing where to begin working against what they saw as the unalterable conditions of systemic class, race, and gender inequality. If, however, capitalism is viewed as the result of a series of decisions and practices being implemented by social agents on many different levels, there are many possible entry points for developing strategies. These professional shelter workers were unable to do this, however, so they instead continued in the role of "fixing" young people.

When someone like Amy or Jacob resisted these efforts, they were not cooperating and, therefore, were easily portrayed as causing their own hardship by being non-compliant. The role of the staff member was understood as offering expert advice on how to fix whatever pathology within the individual teen was causing their personal homelessness. Never did these sheltering professionals have to take the time to develop a relationship with these homeless young people in an effort to find out what they really wanted. As holders of "expert" knowledge, the staff already knew what was needed to help homeless people succeed.

But what about Karen's earnestly expressed sentiment that we have to do what we can to really help these young people who are clearly hurting? Of course staff should help people to survive, but does it really help to work so hard at convincing a young person that the reason they are homeless is because of personal inadequacies within them? Should we really strive to teach these homeless people the needed discipline and subservience to authority needed to "succeed" in alienating and demeaning food-service work? Is a young homeless person like Amy who feels disrespect for values of individualism and materialism ever going to readily agree to such reformative practices? Does it really help to offer skills for working in barely existent middle-class jobs or to obtain non-existent affordable housing? As we've seen over and over again, these efforts are no panacea to ending homelessness.

All of these efforts focused on staff developing tools for uncovering what is inside each subject was the cause of his or her homelessness. Data demonstrating that available jobs in the local setting paid wages inadequate to afford any apartment in the city was understood as something we could do little about, as was the articulated sentiment from some young people that they were homeless because they had a disdain for middle-class American lives.

Interestingly, despite the difficulty that Karen and Elena, the outreach worker, had in getting homeless youth to participate in their groups, several young people in the shelter and living on the streets did become regular participants in two community organizations during the late 1990s. A very active Food Not Bombs chapter organized a food program as well as several political events, and a group called Radical Anarchist Youth put together a film series at the Unitarian Church. Both of these attracted active, regular participation from many of the people refusing more reformative efforts. In 1999, I asked Elena if she had participated in either group as part of her work. She had not done so, but thought it would be a good idea, as she would then have been working with, rather than on, the young homeless people. However, she expressed that she felt her supervisors would not support it: "They'd want to get a little group together or something that they could show to the grant people. I'm mean, I think the grant people wouldn't be so keen on it."

Eventually, when the reformative efforts failed to eliminate the presence of homeless young people in the downtown area, it became clear that much of the community was concerned primarily with the effects of visible poverty on downtown merchants. Young adults panhandling or playing music on the sidewalks in front of city stores were not welcomed by business owners hoping to keep attracting an upscale clientele to the city. In response, new laws were soon passed that banned playing hackeysack in the park, riding bikes or skateboards on sidewalks, and several other activities, all clearly focused on helping consumers feel more comfortable.

Elena expressed this reality very clearly a few weeks before she quit the outreach therapist position. She explained that the majority of homeless young people she worked with tended to be poor black or Puerto Rican kids, girls leaving abusive situations, and pregnant young women. Yet almost all funds and public attention focused on the more visible youth who spent their days in the downtown shopping area. She was discouraged that the focus was clearly on managing public homelessness rather than eliminating the structural violence producing racial and sexual inequalities and domestic violence. As she explained, "It's very frustrating. The obvious answer is that those in power don't really want to end homelessness."

CHAPTER 7

Managing Homelessness

VIN: *"Has there been any effort to organize those on the waiting list or to document the number of those who cannot find shelter as the number of homeless people has increased?"*

GLORIA: *"Organize? No, absolutely not. I don't think so."*

VIN: *"And so what we need to do is work as hard as we can to stuff these people in someplace, anyplace, it doesn't matter where they work or want to live."*

GLORIA: *"Right, they should accept any shelter. As opposed to saying what is happening in society at large that is contributing to the increased numbers of homeless people."*

The previous chapters detailed how sheltering industry practices based on HUD's "continuum of care" produce shelter staff who function to govern homeless people. This chapter explores another way in which people working in shelters respond in ways that fail to decrease homelessness. While they are committed to ending homelessness, the role of many shelter staff members is limited to managing homelessness. When staff are hired and trained to treat disorders of the self they can hardly be expected to offer a collective or political response to homelessness. Although not all staff comply with that description, those who engage in different sorts of practices still must operate within the confines of the "continuum of care" model. If they begin to step too far out of their defined roles and begin challenging systemic conditions, they are putting themselves and the program at risk. As a result, shelter staff continued to manage "the homeless" for the benefit of housed citizens without engaging in practices which might end homelessness.

An Increased Demand for Shelter Beds

Beginning in the winter of 1993–94, there was a dramatic increase in the number of homeless people in Northampton. For the first time, the program was no longer able to consistently provide a bed to all those in need. The initial response was simply to take in everyone needing shelter during the winter months with the hope of moving them to another shelter the next day. This proved difficult, as there were rarely any open beds at other shelters. On some nights as many as ten more people were in the house than beds available.

Shelter staff quickly decided that they did not favor this policy. Donna, Gloria, and Ann all argued that they could not do any of the quality counseling work they were hired, trained, and paid to do with so many people in the building. Donna, in particular, argued that all of the staff time was spent on crisis intervention, breaking up disputes, and doing intakes. Through discussions in staff meetings, we decided that it was unsafe to homeless people to warehouse them in such a manner. A series of solutions was proposed. Administrators and staff documented the increased demand. These numbers were then presented to the Mayor's office, clergy, and the press in an effort to facilitate developing more services. This eventually resulted in the development of a broad-based community effort to organize a winter cot program in churches. In addition, staff began to turn people away while compiling a waiting list for shelter. A consistent waiting list of at least 30–50 people resulted.

ESTABLISHING A WAITING LIST

VIN: *"How do you see the community respond to the increased demand for shelter?"*
GLORIA: *"You mean other than pulling their hair out? Oh, that's a difficult question. Well, in a sense, it seems that we haven't been able to respond proactively because the problems are so great that they're constantly being thrown at. In a sense, it's a crisis mode. It's reactive."*
VIN: *"So, you don't think we've really made any fundamental changes?"*
GLORIA: *"In the way Grove Street is? ... No. I think it's great that we're having interesting staff meetings and we're having those organizing meetings, but fundamental change in the way things are run and what we're doing? I don't see that."*

On a hot July night in 1996, I pulled into the shelter to begin my evening shift. A few guests were in the backyard playing volleyball. Others sat at a table talking, drinking iced tea, and smoking. Among those at the table was Roberto. Roberto, a Puerto Rican man in his mid-40s, had left the previous month after a long stay. Under pressure from Donna and Leopoldina to clear a bed for someone on the waiting list, he moved into a local rooming house.

"Hey, how are you doing?" I asked, hoping that Roberto was not here for a bed because of our long waiting list. I was also pretty sure that he had used up his allotted days for the year.

Roberto answered in a quavering voice: "Not too good, Vin. Can I talk to you?"

Vin: "Sure, I'm supposed to be meeting with Donna soon, but I have a few minutes. What happened?" As we talked, we walked into the shelter. I noticed that Donna and Karen were in the office with the door closed, so I told Roberto that we'd have to talk in the living room.

I was hoping that Roberto had come up to the shelter to talk with me about his family situation. He and his wife had been separated for the past ten months and his life had deteriorated along with their relationship. Since the separation, he'd been living in shelters and biding his time. While staying at the shelter, he would often visit his family on weekends and spent the majority of his disability check on his wife and children. Sunday and Monday evenings would almost always include a long talk as he asked for my help with sorting out his feelings from these visits, especially how to handle his emotions in a non-violent manner.

Roberto, looking at his feet, replied: "I'm trying to see if I can stay here again. I'm desperate. Can you help me? The lady I was sharing a room with was evicted today."

Roberto explained that he'd been sharing a room for the last month at a local SRO with a woman and her boyfriend. As Roberto told the story, her boyfriend took all of her money and spent it on alcohol. Roberto had given all the money he had left after paying his share of the rent to his estranged wife for food for their children. He said that he couldn't leave the area to go to another shelter because he needed, emotionally, to be near his children. "I only get to see my kids once a week now. You know how hard it is for me. I can't be in Springfield or Holyoke and not see them. I'd just fall apart. I really hope I can stay. I have nowhere to go. I need to be close to my kids. They're all I have. I don't get to see them enough as it is, only on weekends."

The problem was that there were 42 people on the waiting list and that Roberto had already stayed for more than 60 days. He asked if he could just stay until August 1, when his next check came, and then he'd get a room. I asked, "But I know that other staff are going to ask how it's going to be any different this time. How do we know you are going to get a room then? What do we do if you give all your money to your family and still don't have a place to live?"

Roberto responded that he needed to get a room. He said that when his wife asked him to leave he decided to give it a year to see if she'd take him back. The year would be up soon and he would try to move on with his life. If he didn't find a room by August 1, he promised he would just leave. "All I'm asking for is a chance. I did good when I was here before. I wasn't kicked out or anything. I helped everyone." Donna and I decided to let him stay the night and discuss his situation at the staff meeting the next day.

We talked more that evening and I told Roberto that I would advocate for him. "I wouldn't worry about it too much. I can't see how we won't let you back in for a month."

Roberto insightfully replied, "You don't have to worry because you're not in my place. I feel like I'm on death row waiting for the hanging judge to make his decision. I have no other place to go. I can't live outside. I need a place where the visiting nurse can give me my medication [visiting nurses came to administer medications to Roberto]. Plus, if I don't have an address, I'll be picked up for violating my parole. Please try to let me stay."

My prediction was wrong. All the other staff at the meeting were against allowing Roberto to return because he had not been working with us on a budget. The best I could work out was that he could be placed on the waiting list and allowed to return when his name came up in a month or so. Leopoldina was emphatic at the staff meeting: "I don't trust him. He lied to me the last time he was here. I don't believe the story about giving money to his wife. I've heard from another guest here that his wife said he never gave her any money. He left the day I asked him to see how he was keeping to his budget."

I replied, "But how do we know she's telling the truth? We're going to not let him stay because of a third-hand story from someone we don't even know? I just feel like we owe him some type of commitment. We worked with him for months and he was doing good work around the house for the month before he left. It seems like we're judging him as not worthy of shelter and I hate that."

Aaron: "But, he wasn't really working with us. The moment we asked about the budgeting he was out of here."

Donna: "He needs to start taking care of himself and setting better priorities. He wasn't able to do that the last time he was here."

I was becoming quite frustrated. "He wasn't able to do it because he's not ready to give up on getting back with his family. Maybe he should move on, but by not giving her his money he'd be admitting that it was over and he's not ready to do that. Of course, he wasn't able to stick with our budget for him because it went against everything he was hoping for. I just don't see what harm it will cause by letting him back for a month."

Leopoldina: "You all forced me into doing these damn budgets as surveillance on people staying here and he didn't live up to it. I'm under all this pressure to fix these people. Structure, structure, structure. If we want this structure, we can't let him back."

Donna and her direct supervisor had told Leopoldina two months previously that she needed to work more effectively with guests. One suggestion was that of budgeting homeless people's limited incomes. When we discovered that it wasn't legal for staff to control a homeless person's money, Donna and Hannah suggested that we simply make the homeless person acquiesce through mandating a budget as a condition of extended stays.

After a few more minutes of the staff conversation, it became apparent that there was little chance of Roberto getting back into the shelter. I was infuriated after the meeting, especially because Leopoldina, my usual ally, had let me down. Karen volunteered to inform Roberto.

I left the shelter after the meeting. Roberto was standing in the backyard crying when I came back. I went over and apologized for what I considered an unjust decision. Roberto, in a halting, choked voice, explained that he'd called his wife and explained the situation to her and begged her to let him stay there for a few days. "She treated me like a dog. She said if I stayed in her house. In her house! That's my house too. She's not treating me with any respect. I'm a man! She just whined about me leaving cigarette butts around. I don't have any choice. I don't know what to do. I have to go there. She doesn't understand."

I volunteered to drive him the 10 miles to his wife's home. During the ride Roberto described the phone call and expressed his shock at the staff decision. "I don't understand. I did so much around there while I was in the transitional bed. I helped out everyone. What more could I have done?" Arriving at the house, I loaned Roberto $3 for cigarettes and left. Roberto slouched off toward his house and his youngest son's greetings with tears streaming down his face.

Later in the week, I came by the shelter to do some administrative work and spoke with Leopoldina. She explained how she went home after the staff meeting feeling very angry. "I feel awful about the Roberto situation. That's all I've been thinking about. I just caved into the pressure for more structure and budgeting."

Vin: "That's why I was arguing so much. I just couldn't understand it. If we want to prevent that from happening, we need to present alternatives and you were supporting it. Everybody else is ready to go right along with the punitive, authoritative model. It's more of staff, as the experts who know best, deciding what the best way of solving that individual's homelessness is and who deserves shelter based on the fucked-up logic of how well they go along with our plan for them. Like we have the answers."

Leopoldina: "I know. I know. I gave in. I just feel like I'm under all this pressure now to show positive outcomes. That's all I ever hear. Structure and outcomes. I have to justify my job and the people staying here lose. The political and self-education gets lost and that's what I value."

Eventually, three weeks later, Roberto made it back into the shelter when his name came up on the waiting list. He and his wife continued to work toward some type of reconciliation. In early September, he moved out to try to stay with some friends. A week later, he called the shelter to put his name on the waiting list once again.

Staff at the shelter have struggled to be fair while it has become routine to turn homeless people away. Of the 75 people who called for a bed during August 1996, only seven ever made it in. This was consistent throughout the year: only 107 of the 261 people trying for a bed from January through September managed to get into the shelter. We decided on a nightly basis to accept 30 to 40 people having no safe place to stay.

When a bed opens at the shelter, staff are faced with the prospect of deciding who gets to move in. Do we take in the 20-year-old pregnant woman, the 25-year-old man working at a local fast-food restaurant, the 17-year-old who was just kicked out of her home, the 38-year-old who is completing a substance-abuse program, the woman who is being battered on a daily basis, the 73-year-old who can not afford local rents on his social security check, or any of the many other people we've come to know? What is the fair way of deciding who must sleep outdoors?

We considered a variety of proposals. Suggested policies included prioritizing those on the waiting list to take the most needy or desperate people, more intensive case management to move people out faster, increasing the number of people in the shelter, letting people stay for one night in the case of "emergencies," decreasing how long people stay at the shelter by being tougher in granting extended stays, or maintaining a strict chronological order of admittance into the shelter. In years of struggling, we could not come up with a policy acceptable to anyone, as all "reasonable" approaches resulted in continued widespread homelessness.

WHO IS MOST DESERVING OF A SHELTER BED?

One particularly interesting approach to responding to the increase in requests for shelter beds was that of prioritizing people on the waiting list. Feeling that it was beyond their ability to decrease the number of people seeking shelter, Hannah and Donna proposed the plan after speaking with shelter administrators and program directors from throughout the state.

The problem with trying to prioritize homeless people came down to an issue for each staff member of trying to determine who was most worthy of being helped. The proposed plan called for the person working to determine which person would cooperate most fully with staff-suggested helping strategies through a brief discussion over the phone and any prior knowledge of that guest from previous shelter stays. In this manner, people would be divided into those worthy of our "help" and those unworthy of a shelter bed. Having 30 or 40 homeless people to choose from would enable the staff to select those people who might "benefit" from their expertise and, in the process, make the program look better to funders through enhancing "outcomes." This policy obviously did nothing to decrease the actual amount of homelessness. The following examples demonstrate how this worked.

At a staff meeting during March of 1996, the waiting list came up for discussion. A man staying at a shelter in Springfield had called the previous night. He wanted to come to Grove Street because he had just regained his overnight shift at a warehouse just north of Northampton. He had no car and, if he worked the shift, he wouldn't be able to sleep indoors, as the Springfield shelter closed for the day. He stated that he'd only need the bed for a few weeks because he would take home over $400 per week with this job and, therefore, could quickly save enough money to get a room. The staff discussed the situation and tried to decide what to do. We were all quite uncomfortable as we grappled over the right thing to do.

Leopoldina: "The problem is that we have 40 or 45 people ahead of him on that waiting list and are we being fair to them?"

Donna: "Well, the other precipitating factor which we might want to consider is that he is a recovering alcoholic and he just got straight again. His boss is willing to give him another chance and give him the job back, but he won't be able to do it if we don't let him in."

Ann: "How long has he been on the waiting list?"

Leopoldina: "He just called for the first time."

Vin: "See, it just doesn't seem fair to all of those people who have been on our waiting list for months trying to get a bed here."

Leopoldina (sarcastically): "Well, actually the last time we tried to get in touch with people we couldn't reach many of them. So, maybe we could think of it as only skipping ahead of ten or fifteen people if that makes us feel better."

Donna: "He has this job and will only be needing the bed for a finite period of time. We could look at it as he already has one of the pieces of the puzzle in place for moving out of homelessness. He is someone we can really help by just giving him a bed."

Leopoldina: "Isn't it fun trying to play god, deciding who is the most worthy of a bed?"

Vin: "That's the problem. I worry about the precedent of deciding who is most worthy based on what "pieces" they have in place already. Do we decide that someone can get a bed because they have a job at Burger King, do we give precedence to someone because they are officially declared disabled so they have preference for subsidized housing, do we let someone who is already on SSI in before someone who is just applying, do we let someone in sooner because they have a housing voucher? We can do that and it will make our "outcome" statistics look much better, but I hope we don't. I think it's a dangerous way of looking at the people we work with."

Leopoldina: "Right, it's an old game of dividing into the worthy and unworthy poor, but what do we do?"

Donna: "We have to make some decision and if we don't let him in he won't be able to get to his job. He really can't stay at any of the other shelters."

Vin: "I see that [his being unable to keep his job if he stayed at any other shelter] as being a more legitimate way of deciding. If distance and not being able to keep your job and stay at any of the other shelters is the deciding factor, I'll agree with that. I just don't want us forcing homeless people to fight with each other for shelter space by posing themselves as more worthy than other people. Plus, I see us as just fighting among ourselves over what to do when the problem and the answer lies outside of just us."

Leopoldina: "We have to consider that we don't have the answer. There might not be a right decision."

After further discussion, we agreed that we would allow this man to stay at the shelter. Donna agreed that we needed more shelter beds in town, but could not fathom how staff practices might address my suggestion that we actually work to decrease and prevent homelessness in the community. The possibility of staff practices aimed at addressing systemic inequality still did not make sense to her or other staff members. Instead, Leopoldina called the homeless man to tell him he had a bed and the other people on the waiting list simply had to stay outside.

Such decisions occurred on almost a daily basis. Not knowing how to help all those needing a place to stay, we would frequently fall back on trying to prioritize the waiting list, but this was a no-win proposition. As the following example describes, it comes down to accepting that there will be many people going without the very basic right of a safe place to sleep. None of us felt that there was any fair, "objective" way of making such a decision, but this concept of "worthiness" continued to surface. Even when people articulated an unwillingness to "prioritize" those on the waiting list, actual practices (including my own) continued to do just that as we had to decide whom to let in on any given day.

By August 1996, we had been discussing the waiting list at least once a month for a year and had yet to agree about anything except our frustration. I had just assembled some of our statistical data and found that only 35 of the 155 people on our waiting list during the first half of the year ever made it into the shelter. Although we told homeless people that we went through the waiting list in order, I found that most of the people who stayed during this time never were on the waiting list. Instead, they were taken into the shelter as "emergencies" through our now routine practice of "prioritizing" who was most worthy.

I wrote a summary of the data in the staff communication book asking the other staff how we should respond. I suggested that I feared it was becoming routine for us to accept turning people away. Nobody responded. When I asked some staff in person, they stated that they just did not know what to do. Others stated that we were doing the best we could.

My prodding had the impact of creating a space at the next staff meeting for another discussion of the waiting list. Karen started by asking if we couldn't just dispense with the waiting list. This was what the nearby family shelter had done, as they found it too depressing to keep track of the families they could not help. Karen suggested that "we decide who to let in as people call if we have any openings and work with them more when they are here."

Donna argued, however, that "one reason we started to keep a waiting list is to help track the increasing numbers of people in need." We used the numbers of homeless people to document the need in the region so that we could do community outreach and approach funders for more services and more money. She recalled how we used the numbers to help push clergy and local politicians to support the winter cot program. After further discussion, Karen and Donna came to a mutual agreement to, in Karen's words, "have a list, but not feel like we have to go by it. I'd like to be able to let someone in when I think they are really needy." Donna agreed: "Right, we can somehow prioritize the list."

When I asked how they proposed determining who was the most needy or the most worthy of a shelter bed, Karen suggested that we simply "develop a telephone intake," and Donna agreed. When Leopoldina and I repeated our belief that all people should have a right to a bed and that we should not be dividing people into who was deserving of a safe place to sleep, Karen asserted that the proper way for staff to respond to homelessness was through developing more effective ways of treating disorders within homeless people. She was supported in this view by Hannah and Rachel, the shelter administrators, and Donna, the director.

Karen again suggested that staff should prioritize people on the waiting list: "Some people are going to use our services more than others. If one person is really going to work with us when they are here and the other people just sit around for two months, I don't see what's wrong with taking the person who we can help the most and not let those other people abuse the place." This idea of abusing the shelter is interesting: those people who would not cooperate with either a self-help program or staff retraining efforts were portrayed as abusing the homeless shelter and, ultimately, undeserving of even a shelter bed. She could not agree at that moment that every person had a right to a place to sleep inside.

Karen also suggested that "we could do a better job of working with the people here and holding them more accountable. We need to work with them right away, even before they come in. We could sit down together and develop a plan for how to work on their issues and how they'd stick with it. Staff would check in with them weekly and, if they aren't sticking to the plan, they'd have to leave. I just think we can do more to help people here. If someone won't work with me, I can't do my job."

Leopoldina argued with Karen's view of the job: "I think our job is to provide housing and change society to end homelessness, not fix or pathologize people."

I asked Karen, "OK, so, what if you have Jacob who decides that what he wants to do during his stay at the shelter is to perfect his volleyball serve and become a better spades player. Does he get an extension?"

Karen: "But that's not going to help him. If that's all he's doing, he's not helping himself. Somebody else could use that bed more."

Vin: "So, we're really deciding once again what people need. They can design their plan as long as we, the great expert source of knowledge, deem it worthy of fixing whatever is wrong with them and makes them homeless. It's just individualizing homelessness again."

Karen: "We have to do something."

Aaron joined in at this point: "Right, we have to do something, but we don't have to continue to blame and promote self-blaming by the people staying here."

Karen, becoming frustrated with the rest of us, pleaded: "Can't we just talk with the people when they call? We could find out from that who needs the place the most."

Robert then spoke up for the first time: "A potential problem with that process is that the person who is most articulate about their needs might be the one who is deemed most worthy. We've all experienced that sometimes those who talk the most are not exactly the one's in the most need. Often, it may very well be the opposite case. Someone may be so traumatized that they cannot advocate for themself and will accept being turned away. We'd have to guard against that occurring."

Leopoldina suddenly sat up and asked, "Do any of you remember the television program *Queen for a Day*?"

Robert, nodding vigorously, replied, "Yes!" (Nobody else recalled the program.)

Leopoldina continued her analogy. "Well they would get these poor woman on this show each week and they had to get up there and say how pathetic their life was. There was this applause meter. The woman who was able to come across as the most pathetic would get the most applause. So, you'd have this woman up there describing how her husband left her, the car was broken down, they had no food, and the electricity was just being shut off. The crowd would go wild and she'd be given this crown to wear and a new refrigerator."

Robert: "Right, and still no food to go in that refrigerator or washer and dryer. It was disgusting."

Leopoldina: "Well, that's what all of this reminds me of. We want the homeless person to get on the phone and tell us how pathetic or worthy of living in a shelter they are."

Donna: "I surely don't want to see us moving in that direction, but we have to do something. We need to come up with a process that is fair for everyone."

Vin: "But, there is no fair way of telling 40 people each day that they don't get to sleep inside that night. That's what I object to, trying to think we can come up with something that's fair. The whole situation is unjust."

Donna, "Let's also keep in mind that we need to be fair to the people staying here and keep the census at a manageable number of consistent guests so we can really help those who are already in the shelter."

Robert, "I agree. Our primary responsibility should be for the 20 people who are in the shelter. We're doing a good job. We're doing the best we can. I think we should acknowledge that."

Vin, "Can I discuss one concrete case because I promised someone last night that we'd have an answer for him tonight? Domingo called again last night and was desperately pleading with me to get him into the shelter. He's working three jobs in Amherst and staying with friends and co-workers while he tries to save up money for a room or apartment. He's been on our waiting list for close to a month and he said he can't stay with his friends much longer."

Leopoldina (laughing): "The applause meter is shooting right up. Can you make him a little more desperate and maybe we can give him a bed?"

All of the staff were struggling with how to manage the situation. The response of some was to try to confine their job to "helping" the few homeless people who managed to make it into the shelter. After a lengthy discussion, we agreed to let Domingo stay. Aaron agreed because we could not get in touch with anyone ahead of him on the waiting list, but Donna and Karen based their decision on the fact that he was working several jobs and should, therefore, be a higher priority for a shelter bed.

Leopoldina and I disagreed with that view, but we were largely ineffective in changing staff practices toward challenging the systemic inequities we believed were causing the increased numbers of homeless people. We were stuck making daily decisions regarding who was allowed to sleep indoors.

Leopoldina's argument about *Queen for a Day* proved somewhat persuasive, however. Robert and Donna eventually agreed not to follow Karen's suggestion of disregarding the waiting list. A compromise policy was agreed upon. After deciding that there was no fair way of deciding who was most worthy, we tried maintaining a waiting list based solely on when someone first called for a bed. When a bed became available, the staff would work down the waiting list calling each name in order. Exceptions could be made only in the case of perceived dire physical emergencies, such as domestic violence.

This method soon proved unsatisfactory, as most homeless people did not have a cellular phone with them on the street or even a friend who could take a message. Additionally, we realized that we were still simply managing a small segment of the homeless population and, by doing little to prevent or end homelessness, we continued to be confronted with a large waiting list.

FIRST COME, FIRST SERVED

Raymond, the former guest I discussed previously, came by the shelter one evening. He called out, "Hey Vinny, is there an open bed here?"

Vin: "No, unfortunately we have this giant waiting list, but let me check what I can do."

We had no open beds and 53 names on the list. "Well, there are a ton of people ahead of you on the list so I don't think it would be fair to let you in ahead of them. Do you need the bed for just this one night or for awhile?"

Raymond: "I'll need a place for a little while. My wife just went back into the hospital. She's doing very badly. I've spent the last five years of my life taking care of her and now she's in the hospital and I'm homeless again. Isn't there a couch or any place I can stay?"

Vin: "I just can't. We just had a big discussion at the staff meeting about that and the decision was made not to let people stay on couches. I don't know. We have these tents that were donated and I could give you one of these." In a move of desperation earlier that summer, we had put out a public call for tents to house some of the people unable to get into the shelter.

Raymond: "Ok, can I just set it up out in the yard?"

Vin: "Unfortunately, no. We have to be very careful, the city government got really mad when we even asked for tents this summer. So, we can't let people stay here. There's a place around the corner in the woods where some people have set up tents before and weren't harassed though."

Raymond ate some dinner, took the tent and some blankets, thanked me, and went to sleep outside. He was lucky. He was given a bed at the shelter three weeks later. Two days after entering the shelter he had a full-time job and was registered for a nurses' aide training course.

The way Raymond responded to the lack of beds was far from unique. It was very rare for a person to become angry or upset. I am no longer even surprised when a homeless person willingly accepts not being allowed to sleep on an empty couch. Raymond, however, surprised me. He was usually such a vocal advocate for social justice and I had developed a very close relationship with him over the past three years, yet he meekly accepted a pup tent as a legitimate housing option. I felt awful, but Raymond appeared resigned to the policy.

One guest described this phenomenon: "By the time you get to that point you are so used to having the door slammed in your face that you develop a sense of hopelessness. I think a lot of people figure that's it, oh well, there's nothing I can do. You are so beaten down by the system and you're so beaten down by circumstances that.... The same thing would happen to anyone if they couldn't find shelter night after night after night. They might be angry for awhile, but then they'd just be despairing."

Whether it is fear, despair, or resignation, homeless people seemingly accept being placed on a waiting list. The shelter staff, however, struggled to come up with a system that was equitable and fair while they too accepted the large numbers of homeless people as a "social reality."

RESPONDING WITH SHORTER SHELTER STAYS

ANN: *"We are not working in a setting where challenging systemic issues is valued. There's no room for that. You have to push against a brick wall to even bring it up."*

In addition to our efforts with the waiting list, the staff tried other methods to manage the increased demand for beds. Questions about how long someone should be able to stay at the shelter was a different strategy employed to deal with increasing homelessness. Several staff suggested that if we worked more effectively with people while they were at the shelter, they would be able to solve the problems causing their homelessness. Some argued that we should limit the amount of time any person stayed to a few weeks unless the homeless person was clearly working on "their issues." Once again, the role of staff was defined as limited to that of expert reformers of pathologies within deviant homeless individuals.

We discussed Howard's situation at a staff meeting during November 1995. Howard, the African-American man in his early 20s discussed in Chapter Two, had been working as a cashier at Stop and Shop for several months, but only made about $100 per week from his job. He had been trying to find a shared living situation, but he had not yet been able to arrange any and his time at the shelter was ending.

Donna suggested that, in order to get a further extension, Howard needed a detailed plan to find housing and increase his income. Donna and Robert suggested that Howard be approached and told that he needed to get a second job. Additionally, Donna suggested that Leopoldina work more closely with Howard on developing a budget and budgeting skills. Leopoldina and I expressed our displeasure at the suggestion that the solution to Howard's continued homelessness was teaching him how to better budget his take-home pay. Howard was a very intelligent man with exceptional math skills, as shown by his being admitted to the competitive engineering program at the University of Massachusetts and completing two years of studies before having to leave school. I suggested that the explanation for Howard's financial difficulties might not lie within him, but rather with the decisions being made by his employer not to offer full-time hours. We also pointed out how, based on many prior examples, it was nearly impossible for someone at the shelter to maintain two part-time food-service jobs as scheduling conflicts would inevitably ensue.

Leopoldina argued, "There is only so far that you can budget $90 a week. The problem is a lack of a living wage"

Donna: "But we need to do something. I've had low-paying jobs before and learned that you need to stretch the money and live within a budget." Eventually, because Howard was a friendly, intelligent person who could advocate for himself quite well, all the staff agreed to let him stay longer. Other homeless people who are not so skilled at interpersonal negotiation have been asked to leave the shelter. For example, one man, Roberto, left the shelter after his pleas for an extension were turned down. He began to stay with friends and spent some nights outside. He would stop by the shelter on nights I worked and beg me to help him get into a rooming house. Nor did I ever hear any other staff wonder how Hector, another guest, was doing or if they could help him in the six months after he was asked to leave the shelter. The fact that Hector was now living outside and routinely being picked up by the police was portrayed as his fault. He was homeless because he was portrayed as untrustworthy and unwilling to work with staff. When there are consistently 40 people trying to get in the shelter, it is relatively easy to dismiss anyone whom staff do not like or trust.

ANOTHER ATTEMPT AT MANAGING THE WAITING LIST

While I was working at the shelter one night in September 1996, three people contacted me trying to get into the shelter. Elijah, an African-American man who had been on our waiting list for eight months, was staying at a nearby Veterans Administration hospital, but needed to leave the next day. He was number 33 on the waiting list. I told him that I'd see what happened, but I doubted we would be able to help him.

Enrique was number 72 on the waiting list. Enrique, a Puerto Rican man in his mid 70s, had been at the shelter for a few days over the last two years. He normally lived illegally in his daughter's subsidized apartment. When the landlord threatened her with eviction, he had to leave. He had come to the shelter a few days before and, because several guests were out for the weekend visiting sick relatives, he was told he could stay until Monday.

The third person pleading for a bed was new on the list. She was a 17-year-old woman living in the park. She worked part-time in a shop downtown and had been homeless for about two months. I explained that it would be quite a wait before a bed became available, but to keep in touch.

In addition to these people, three other people I know very well were desperately hoping for beds as soon as possible. Jacob and Dana were two ex-guests of the shelter who had left in July to live with a friend. Unfortunately, that hadn't worked out. They had been living outside again for the last two weeks, and Dana was 4 months pregnant. They had been sleeping in a church doorway but were recently told they could no longer stay there.

The final person seeking a bed was Henry, an 18-year-old who had stayed in the shelter for well over 100 days during the past year. At first, his plan was to somehow finish his last year at high school while living in the shelter, but that never worked out. He then worked at a local fast-food restaurant for almost six months hoping to save money for housing, but that hadn't worked out either. Finally, he moved to a program in nearby Greenfield for homeless people between the ages of 18 and 21. That didn't work out, though, because he quickly felt isolated in Greenfield, away from his friends and family, and soon began to break their rules about drug and alcohol use. He was asked to leave that program in August and had been staying with friends and family and on the street since then while trying to stay sober so he could get back into the youth program. Henry called the shelter that night to beg for a bed. He said he was scheduled to go back to the youth program in a few weeks. He was staying with his mother but did not feel safe there. He was hoping to try to stay clean, but he did not seem able to do so.

None of those people made it into the shelter that night, although four of them did within the next month. The decisions that needed to be made that night were no different than those confronting all of the shelter staff on a nightly basis for the past two years. The staff had been trying their best to come up with a way to manage homelessness, but to little avail.

The situations detailed above exemplify the gut-wrenching, emotionally draining situations facing staff and guests at the shelter on a daily basis. These examples provide insight into the multifaceted dynamics confronting staff as they try to manage the growing demand for sheltering services. A few years earlier we were presented with the situation of too many people needing shelter beds. Our initial response was to take in as many people as came to the door. Some nights we had as many as 30 people, with many sleeping on couches. It was horrible, with constant fighting, distrust, and bickering. The staff decided that there must be an alternative to the apparent choices of accepting that or letting people sleep outside. We tried prioritizing the waiting list, more effective case management, and other strategies within the shelter.

What is apparent from these efforts at managing the homelessness problem are the severe lack of resources in the community and the thoughtful, well-intentioned efforts of the shelter staff to cope with this social problem. These staff members are all very thoughtful, caring, dedicated workers who feel great sympathy and empathy for the homeless people they work with. They all struggle to do the best they can, but within the reality of perceived available choices. Most of those choices, though, involved accepting as a given that there would be homeless people needing shelter. Creating a community without homelessness appeared entirely unreasonable. As a result, when I critically engaged these staff members and forced them to consider the number of homeless people who were being overlooked by their practices, my argument was often rejected in favor of doing "good work" within the shelter. Once staff members accept the fact that it is their duty simply to diagnose and treat disorders within homeless people, it seems that the best they can do is manage the problem through prioritizing, increasing resources, increasing shelter beds, cutting down on stays, or developing strategies to move people out more quickly. No other options seem reasonable. The fact that over 400 people each year are in need of a shelter in a fairly prosperous city of 30,000 people goes largely unchallenged. That has become a normal part of life that as a staff member, homeless person, community activist, or local policy maker one is supposed to believe cannot be changed. Instead, staff struggle with trying to manage the homeless people who need shelter beds.

Alternative strategies for responding to homelessness are possible, however. These were not the only efforts attempted in Northampton. As the next chapter explores in more detail, my engaging in critical dialogues with the people with whom I was working sometimes led to the production of new thinking and new practices. As some of the staff began to be unhappy doing their prescribed jobs of managing homelessness and reforming homeless individuals, alternative practices began to emerge. For example, we began to use data from the waiting list to make an argument to the Mayor's office, community members, and local clergy for more shelter beds. Out of these discussions, a broad coalition of community members came together in "The Next Step Housing Coalition." Leopoldina, Donna, Rachel, and I worked with this group to develop a broad strategy to end homelessness over the next several years. Out of this coalition, an emergency cot shelter was started the next winter. In subsequent years, several new affordable housing units were created in the community. Simply creating more shelter and more affordable housing, however, is not an answer in itself, as many of the structural inequalities producing homelessness within the vast wealth of the United States remain unaltered.

CHAPTER 8

Reflections on an Engaged Ethnography

Effects of the Discourses of Deviancy and Self-Help

The years of ethnographic work described in the preceding chapters uncovered a number of dynamics within the homeless sheltering industry. The recent growth of homelessness coincides with broad-based socio-economic changes, particularly the rising dominance of neoliberal conceptualizations and practices. As a result, the number of people living in poverty and the degree of economic inequality in the United States have steadily increased since the early 1970s. Corporate management has been awarded huge pay increases while enacting policies contributing to corporate downsizing, increased poverty, and homelessness nationally and globally. Additionally, a decline in government and private-sector support led to a shortage of affordable housing units. It is fairly uncomplicated to suggest a correlation between elevated inequality, a scarcity of affordable housing, and homelessness.

However, most efforts to respond to homelessness do not address those systemic processes. Instead, many responses combine punitive legislation with support for "normalization" efforts. Likewise, organized resistance against systemic inequality by homeless people, shelter staff, or homeless advocates is often quite elusive. To understand this seeming consent, it is imperative to contemplate both the material conditions contributing to homelessness and the discursive processes through which social inequality and homelessness have become accepted as "normal." To do this, I examined the routine practices by which HUD's "continuum of care" guidelines have been enacted as "helping" efforts within the sheltering industry in one community.

Through engaging ethnographically with shelter staff, homeless people, shelter administrators, and concerned local advocates, I analyzed how they understand and respond to homelessness. To understand the process of homelessness, it is important to contemplate the subtle, insidious nature of conditions taken for granted as normal, natural, or uncontestable. These structures of inequality are often fashioned in the absence of more coercive tools of domination. Understanding homelessness then becomes a question of analyzing hegemonic processes. Drawing together both Gramscian and Foucauldian analytical tools, I focused on the role that everyday, hegemonizing shelter language and practices play in the discursive production of homeless and housed subjectivities.

153

I uncovered a hypothesis of deviancy dominating within the homeless sheltering industry. Based on produced prototypical conceptions of "the homeless," discourses of self-help and bio-medicalization combine to reproduce a conceptual framework within which homelessness is understood as the result of shortcomings within homeless people. Instead of thinking of "homeless" as being a person without a home, many people understand "homeless" through these prototypical images and related anecdotal examples.

My interest in this work was not so much focused on whether the prototypical images were "real" or accurate. Instead, my interest was in how those images were produced through industry practices and what the effects of these understandings are in terms of limiting responses, policies, and treatments for homelessness. I found that thoughts and actions aimed at "fixing" and "normalizing" homeless people came to make sense to people connected to the shelters while critiques of systemic issues were considered unrealistic or misguided. Dominant practices focused on developing techniques of detecting, diagnosing, and treating disorders within individual homeless people. This is hardly surprising, given that social problems ranging from credit-card debt to depression are currently widely understood as the result of disorders of the individual self and that much of the funding for sheltering programs comes out of HUD's "continuum of care" model. However, this "common-sense" way of understanding and responding to the social problem of homelessness has had several effects.

Perhaps most prominently, shelter language and "helping" practices operate as techniques of self making. Routine shelter practices train homeless people to look for and treat disorders within themselves. Subjectivities are created through the languages of self-empowerment and self-improvement and practices of diagnosing and treating homeless deviants. Self-governing homeless subjects are often produced. These self-blaming and self-governing people can, furthermore, scarcely be expected to spend time developing strategies for collectively resisting systemic inequities.

Not all homeless people, however, comply with the dominant languages and practices of self-reform. Some homeless people, like Ariel and Raymond, actively resist efforts to treat or govern them. Other people learn that they are rewarded for cooperating and punished for "being difficult." On the surface, their behavior may be read as quite compliant. Their resistance against the staff and community members' "helping" practices and the discursive production of homeless people as deviant remains confined to the grumblings and rule breaking that James Scott referred to as "hidden transcripts" (1990). Non-compliant homeless people must still operate within the dominant medicalizing discourse. As a result, many non-compliant people practice individualized resistance against shelter "helping" efforts. If someone, as in the case of Raymond, sees a need to challenge social inequality, their resistance remains an individual struggle. As a result, homeless people are not likely to offer collective resistance against structural violence.

I also examined how discursive practices define the role of shelter staff. In my experiences, most people working in homeless shelters are very committed to ending homelessness. However, they also do not function outside the neoliberal "continuum of care" discourses. I analyzed staff hiring procedures, the development of job descriptions, staff training, and the development of a staff conduct policy in addition to daily case-management and surveillance practices. Discursive practices produce shelter staff whose primary function is defined within the narrow parameters of being "helping professionals." To work in a shelter often requires specialized expertise in governing and managing homeless people.

Finally, the sheltering industry serves as an apparatus for reinforcing and reifying dominant discursive understandings about homelessness. Popular conceptions of "the homeless" as deviant people requiring treatment and personal "development" both guide the "continuum of care" model and are, in turn, reinforced through resultant shelter practices. Much well-meaning effort is expended in these "helping" efforts by people within the sheltering industry. Hundreds of millions of dollars and tens of thousands of labor hours are annually devoted to detecting deviancy and training homeless people in the hope of resolving homelessness. Yet, by failing to address systemic and discursive inequities, these efforts remain ineffective in decreasing homelessness. Education, life-skills training, and self-improvement efforts are of little real value without collective political movements making existing jobs pay living wages. Similarly, efforts to create more affordable housing, while possibly being a solution to homelessness, will do nothing to eliminate poverty without social movements aimed at denaturalizing current dominant discourses about the "rights" of capital and redistributing the nation's wealth in a more equitable fashion. As a result, the well-meaning, helping practices lead to a wealth of time and money spent on efforts to manage homelessness and govern the homeless, but this does virtually nothing to eradicate homelessness.

Engaging with Local Actors: Embodying an Activist, Oppositional Position

Once we understand these dynamics, though, how can we use this knowledge? To return to the questions posed in the introduction, what do you do with these insights? How can our ethnographic understandings help us work politically against the material conditions of homelessness or the discursive production of "the homeless" as deviant types?

Several possible ethnographic interventions exist. On one level, anthropologists may produce written material that engages dominant conditions by becoming part of the public dialogue about the social problem. Examples of this type of work abound. They range from the engaged anthropological work found in Anna Lou Dehavenon's frequent written reports and press releases detailing the conditions of homelessness and the inadequacies of New York City's sheltering programs (1993) to the moving accounts of poverty and structural inequality detailed in Jonathon Kozol's books (1995; 1991). While acknowledging the strength of that work, my engagement also took an additional form. I began to understand the problem as one of how to critically engage hegemonic understandings and practices. I did this through actively engaging the well-meaning people I was working with in critically examining our efforts against homelessness.

The hegemony of the bio-medical discourse made some practices and understandings appear as common sense and normal while marginalizing other possibilities. Yet any hegemony is never totalizing. Clearly, Raymond, Ariel, Anthony, Ann, Gloria, Leopoldina, Maria, and Jonathan were not completely dominated by the "continuum of care" model. Yes, as witnessed by this work, counter- and alter-hegemonic practices are often quite effectively marginalized by a variety of discursive and structural means. Peripheral discourses allow alternative conceptions and practices to emerge, but to do so requires politically committed activist work. Even then, there are no guarantees of success.

The objective of my research became one of engaging dialogically with homeless people and shelter staff in an effort to come to new understandings that might make it conceptually possible for new actions to emerge. My strategy involved analyzing and engaging with the well-meaning agents within this growing industry to problematize routine and taken-for-granted understandings and practices. My ethnographic method came to entail an explicitly articulated oppositional point of view. I began to both problematize the effects of routine shelter practices and to discuss with staff, guests, and the local press information and points of view that had previously been marginalized locally in the activist hope of creating space for alternative understandings and practices to emerge.

My multi-positioned status as academic researcher, shelter staff member, activist for socio-economic change, and advocate for the rights of homeless people allowed me to both embody and voice these views in an oppositional, yet collegial, manner. This both allowed me to engage social actors in critically evaluating our "common sense" understandings and practices and directed local responses to homelessness on new courses.

By advocating an activist ethnographic engagement with those you are studying, I am not suggesting that an anthropologist is an expert who enlightens through teaching the misinformed. At several points, I had to reiterate to both staff and homeless people that I did not have all the answers. In fact, when I began this work, I very much practiced actions based on the deviancy model myself as I approached my goal of helping homeless people with missionary zealousness. Homelessness is a complex social phenomenon. What I could do was utilize my ethnographic work to prompt all of us (including myself) to think in new ways and pose new questions about homelessness in all its complexity. These efforts took place on many levels. It first involved documenting concrete practices, analyzing how the practices make sense to the people involved, uncovering effects of such routine behaviors in terms of the construction of homeless, institutional, and staff subjectivities, and, finally, working together to develop new ways of thinking and acting within the industry and beyond.

This was not easy. As I engaged with shelter staff, homeless people, and local advocates in critiquing our practices on the local level, a commonly articulated concern was that such an analysis is potentially politically debilitating. Staff now joined homeless guests in feeling resigned to established practices. Ann summarized this point quite nicely: "You have to give people some hope. It works well to think of homelessness as being individualized and deviant. Then you can work on fixing the individual problem. The solutions are easy for both the staff and guests. You try more services, a different counselor, more AA meetings, or a different job. If you try to tell them to think of themselves and homelessness in a new way, they can very easily feel stuck and hopeless. It's overwhelming when you think of needing to make systemic changes."

Leopoldina voiced similar sentiments: "You're right, but I feel like a deer with its head caught in the headlights…. Such critical thinking is crazy making. People just don't want to hear it. I know we need to do everything differently, but I just don't know what to do. It's just so overwhelming."

Guests at the shelter often respond similarly. One homeless woman, Susan, stated, "Yes, what you say makes sense. Of course the problems are with the economy. I'm not stupid, but thinking about changing the wage structure or getting more housing is just too much. I have no idea of where to even start. I only have so much time here and I have to figure out how to cope with the reality of the situation."

I found that establishing an awareness and mode of action outside set parameters is often seen as too overwhelming. "Helping" professionals often consider this sense of too much awareness as a way of numbing their own professional agency. In an interview with Duccio Trombadori, Michel Foucault describes a similar reaction to his book *Discipline and Punish: The Birth of the Prison*. After years working with agents within the penal institution, "when the book came out, various readers—particularly prison guards, social work-ers, etc.—gave this singular judgement: 'It is paralyzing. There may be some correct observations, but in any case it certainly has its limits, because it blocks us, it prevents us from continuing our activities'" (Foucault 1991: 41).

Reactions similar to this occurred in Northampton. Such articulations of frustration, however, became a goal of mine; I saw them as an entry point for further engagement. Given the dominance of the bio-medical model, the rise of neoliberalism, and the perception of neoliberal globalization as a totalizing, all-encompassing system, it is not surprising that shelter staff, homeless people, and policy makers often have difficulty conceiving of what else they can do. When they do attempt to transcend these discursive limits and dare to undertake new practices, they are often disciplined right back into their assigned professional roles. This happened in Northampton. The fear of lost relative privileges and middle-class status caused some staff members to silence themselves when they were threatened for experimenting with new ideas and staff practices.

An initial reaction to this analysis by many of those I worked with was to feel that they could no longer work within the defined parameters of the sheltering industry. Karen stated, "From what you're saying it seems like we should all quit these jobs and do something that would really change things." That is one possibility. Ann and Gloria eventually took this path in leaving the shelter to form a community center where they hoped to work more cooperatively with formerly homeless people. Donna hoped to accomplish a similar goal through her graduate-school education. But leaving the sheltering industry is not the only possibility.

Other staff and guests at the shelter began questioning practices with the hope of developing new strategies. This was difficult and time-consuming work. However, as a result it became nearly impossible for the service providers and many of the homeless people I worked with to blindly continue practices focused on fixing deviant individual homeless people. This was not an emotionally easy process and it was met with resistance on many fronts. However, an opportunity for rethinking and redefining homelessness and ourselves opened up.

What I proposed was an alternative between normalizing perceived pathological homeless people and simply accepting homelessness. As I advocated for the rights of homeless people in the shelter and in the community, I urged those within the sheltering industry to devote time and resources to work with real people in their own locations and to alter the governing practices within the shelters. The staff could become advocates and allies working together with homeless people rather than reinforcing a constructed dichotomy between expert professional reformers and deviant, pathological victims in need of treatment.

Previously accepted restrictions on what is possible and acceptable for both staff and homeless guests can be stretched and challenged. Shelter staff and homeless people can learn to re-think their established and habitual roles, including how they work with each other and the broader community. Staff can become allies and advocates for homeless people, rather than simply being engaged in their surveillance, monitoring, and reform. Preliminary discussions began to take place at this shelter on such practices as developing and enforcing shelter rules, how to fund the shelter without being beholden to state welfare agencies, who has access to producing the official summary of guest behavior in the daily logs, how intakes are conducted, what statistical and demographic information is compiled, and how such data are conveyed to both the local community and government sources. New practices and resistance strategies aimed at altering both the material and discursive dimensions of homelessness became possible.

An additional mechanism for engaging people was to offer statistical, ethnographic or demographic data that were not part of the popular discourse in the community or in the shelter. I began to document and talk about these data in a wide variety of settings. Staff meetings, community fora, interactions with clergy and local political leaders, volunteer recruitment efforts, providing reporters with newspaper stories, informal discussions at the shelter, academic meetings, and a shelter newsletter — these all provided opportunities to publicly discuss the systemic and discursive conditions of homelessness. For example, I began to compile and publicize statistical data on previously ignored employment and housing costs as well as ethnographic stories about the difficulty of working one's way out of homelessness within prevailing labor and housing markets.

In addition, I engaged people through sharing the struggles of homeless people to locate income and decent housing. None of the statistical records or grant writing at the shelter included any of this information until I compiled it for my research. Once I shared these efforts, however, it became quite clear to many people that employment, income, and availability of affordable housing were issues to be addressed. Guests and staff began to discuss how they could work cooperatively in actions aimed at altering local wages and housing costs.

We began by focusing on the employment experiences of people at the shelter. Despite some popularly held beliefs about the laziness or learned dependence of "the homeless," many of the people I worked with were desperate to locate jobs and income. Many others were involved in training programs or self-reform to prepare for work. The stories of Howard, Jerry, Ariel, Jenny, Maria, and Ariel were publicized in various public fora and within the shelter in the hope of producing both different understandings about homelessness and new industry practices.

After sharing stories about the working homeless and being shown the data, community members began to consider what they could do differently. This engagement had some effects, but did not lead to what I considered transformative resistance efforts. Overall, initial local responses fell into two categories: on the one hand, an emphasis on luring manufacturing jobs to the area and assisting existing employers to continue operating locally; on the other hand, renewed efforts to enhance the human capital of potential workers through "developing" homeless people while increased services attempted to help them cope with the "reality" of the local situation through training. The proposed solution embraced neoliberal notions with a focus on expanding the ability of individual people to better compete in the market. Suggested remedies included attending the local skill center, accessing public education, developing a mentoring program, and trying for a second job. Staff worked with guests on such "common sense" strategies as how to present oneself at an interview, writing résumés, and budgeting income.

These new practices still focused on changing behaviors or characteristics within homeless people. None really addressed issues of the cost of housing or wages paid in the jobs that existed in the community where homeless people work. For example, there was no effort to turn food-service jobs into good jobs. Therefore, I began to situate ethnographic examples within an historical context of socio-economic changes and housing costs nationally and within the region.

When they were presented with this new analysis, it became more difficult for staff, guests, and policy makers to simply understand the inability of homeless people to obtain jobs paying enough to afford housing as simply the result of individual shortcomings and inadequacies within homeless people. In fact, when I provided shelter staff, shelter administrators, and members of the city planning department with these economic data, they all expressed shock. As one city planner responded, "It changed the way I have to think. I'm just learning about homelessness and I never thought of it in those terms before. You're right. All the programs we've been funding work to treat individual homeless people, as though that was the solution to homelessness, but that's all the information I was given."

This had some effect. Some of these people began to develop new strategies, languages, and practices. Weekly meetings began to take place at the shelter. Homeless people, staff, formerly homeless people, and community members began to discuss how they could work collectively to address homelessness. These meetings quickly focused on two main topics: wages available in local jobs and the cost of housing. After much hard work, outreach and coalition building, two broad-based movements aimed at addressing housing and income developed in the city. A "living wage" campaign, which was initiated within the shelter, gained the support of over 25 labor, youth, community, and religious organizations in planning actions aimed at significantly increasing wages for all low-waged workers in the city. Unlike other US cities that began "living wage" campaigns in the mid-1990s focused only on the wages of workers falling under city contracts, Northampton's effort took a different form. It was rooted in oppositional efforts by some staff and guests within the shelter to remedy the fact that many working poor were homeless in Northampton despite the large profits of their employers. We put much effort into planning and launching the local "living wage" campaign. A remarkable coalition of homeless people, clergy, students, youth activists, union members, social-service workers, and welfare-rights activists began to cooperate toward this goal by early 1997.

Concurrently, a second coalition began to work on securing sites for affordable housing in the community. The impetus for this group also came out of the discussions about housing cost and availability at the shelter meetings. The coalition subsequently developed into a much broader group involving clergy, tenants' associations, homeless people, and concerned volunteers in negotiations with the mayor and governor's office about available land in the city for housing. These advocacy and organizing efforts have continued and have created increased housing options.

This is just a sample of the types of resistance efforts possible when agents within the sheltering industry begin critically evaluating their routine understandings and practices. For these fledgling efforts to become dominant, however, would necessitate a complete restructuring of shelter practices. Languages used, case-management techniques practiced, and statistical representations produced within the shelter could focus on the collective experience of homelessness. Shelter staff and local advocates could work as allies and co-workers with people living on the streets and in the shelters. Staff, shelter administrators, and local clergy could utilize their privileged position of access to the press and local political leaders to advocate for the need to decrease structural inequality rather than the need for more counselors to "fix," govern or manage homeless people. With these practices, a different type of subjects might be produced within the homeless sheltering industry. A renewed possibility of working together to challenge systemic inequality in the community might develop, but not if routine practices continue to detect, diagnose, and treat deviancy among "the homeless."

Of course, social problems like homelessness are not just a result of the deviancy hypothesis. Dominant conceptual frameworks may dictate how subjects understand and respond to social inequities. Thus, new knowledge may produce new kinds of subjects who undertook different resistance strategies aimed at altering structural conditions such as housing cost, housing availability, wage scales, labor laws, health insurance, or racial inequality. Yet, even if changes in conceptual understandings produce new actions, that would be just the start of the struggle. Such a change in actions for the sheltering industry would not come without risks or costs. Local donors and funding agencies who are quite willing to provide money for outreach workers, counselors, and job training programs might not support efforts aimed at altering the social processes of production and distribution of wealth and resources. Shelter administrators might not be able to rely on the local business community, HUD, or the National Institute for Mental Health to fund the shelter. As staff begin to experiment with new ways of responding to homelessness, they might indicate that they do not want the industry to move in an oppositional direction. In fact, this happened in Northampton as funders, political leaders, and administrators responded to our first steps at increased political work around homelessness by threatening future funding.

The Suppressive Role of Funding

HANNAH: *"I sure got this message that we're at risk of losing funding if it's too radical at the shelter."*

DONNA: *"What's become very clear over the last few years is the need to find alternative ways of funding the shelter if we ever want to do more proactive work. That's why I really think we need to explore entrepreneurial ventures out of the house. To get out from under the control of the politicians and granting agencies. It's not that I want to have little capitalist ventures here, but I just don't see how we can do the real political work that needs to take place if we remain beholden to the good will of the local politicians for our funding."*

One further factor that limits social actors' response to the growth of homelessness is the need to fund programs. As became increasingly clear to the shelter staff as we problematized our practices, relying on traditional funding sources often prevented working against systemic inequalities if we wanted to continue to keep our jobs and receive money for the program.

The Grove Street Inn began in 1991 in response to a building take-over and political pressure from local clergy, social activists, and homeless people. Since its inception, the shelter has constantly struggled for financial survival. The agency overseeing the program made a decision to close it due to a lack of funds in 1991 and again in 1995. This action was averted through last-minute donations from two wealthy Northampton residents in 1991 and through a commitment of state funding for the shelter in 1995. In both instances the public appeals for funding were meticulously directed and controlled by Hannah. Using her "expert knowledge" about fundraising and lobbying, even in this desperate moment she hoped to make sure no staff or homeless person offended any potential donor and all requests went through appropriate channels. As staff and guests saw two nearby shelters close when their appeals went unheeded, the possibility of the shelter closing was very real. Consequently, any action that might alienate a potential donor or granting source was seen as risking both one's job and the future of the shelter. Even if this was not the case, the perception of great risk was strong enough to curtail an activist impulse among most staff and suppress most expressions of discontent among homeless people.

Within this climate, Hannah explored a number of potential funds for the program. As the shelter did not receive adequate state or federal funding in the first few years, it relied primarily on the good will of local donors. Hannah's courting of the Downtown Business Association was a key tactic in this effort. Often a few carefully selected shelter guests were chosen to speak to these business leaders about the quality work being done at the shelter to reform their pathologies. The city government showed absolutely no willingness to fund the shelter to any large degree, but did provide some federally funded Community Development Block Grants. Further funding attempts involved applications for grants from private foundations and from state and federal government agencies.

As the earlier discussion surrounding the shelter HUD grant applications makes clear, these funding sources relinquish money only with clearly defined parameters specifying how the money will be used. They most often fund programs that will focus on helping homeless people through improved case management to reform homeless individuals. The only successful HUD sheltering-grant application in Northampton occurred in 1996 when funding was provided to help with job training and job-readiness rehabilitation for homeless people.

Similar dynamics occurred when a grant application was submitted to the Robert Woods Johnson Foundation to help pay for the winter cot program. The hope was to get money to pay for a coordinator for the cot program who would train and supervise volunteers, facilitate the community group, and coordinate the overall running of the cot program. Our application stressed large-scale community involvement in the cot program. We particularly emphasized the hundreds of volunteers who helped to make the shelter work. At a May 1996 meeting it was announced that the Robert Woods Johnson Foundation had asked us to resubmit the application with some adjustments. The most significant suggestion by the grant officers at the foundation was that we add the need for 12 "mentors" to work with guests staying at the cot program. These mentors would add a more programmatic, case-management-like aspect to the cot program and ensure that the program did more than simply provide shelter. Providing shelter was clearly not deemed to be an economical investment. To be fundable, a sheltering program must have a mechanism in place to fix and normalize perceived deviance within homeless people. The mentors were expected to model the behaviors that would enable homeless people to become independently housed.

During fiscal year 1995–1996, the state government provided substantial funding for the shelter. This was made possible through extensive lobbying by Hannah, the mayor's office, HUD officials, and local state legislators. We soon found out that this money did not come without strings attached either. Two events during the spring of 1996 made this abundantly clear.

The Grove Street Inn is located on the property of an old state mental institution. The Northampton State Hospital was closed during a period of widespread deinstitutionalization in the state. As a result, all of our discussions about a lack of shelter beds and the shortage of affordable housing in the city took place in a setting where we could look out the window and see 300 acres of land and several houses sitting empty for years. These empty houses deteriorated as state and city officials decided what to do with the former state hospital property. As the shelter's present location was obtained as a result of negotiations after a building takeover, at meetings the staff and guests frequently raised the subject of using the same tactic as a means of drawing attention to the need for more shelter space and affordable housing. Gloria and Ann, in particular, would return to the shelter for these meetings in an attempt to organize current homeless guests around the idea of a building takeover. Everyone at these meetings expressed potential support for such actions, but Hannah and Rachel were quite explicit in their role as shelter administrators that no staff could take part in such actions in their role as shelter staff. They were very concerned with potential strained relations with funders if staff stepped outside of their assigned roles.

Finally, on April 15, 1996, a former guest at the shelter, David, and fellow local activists (primarily student "Food Not Bombs" members from Hampshire College) took over one of the abandoned buildings on the state hospital grounds under the name of The Northampton Restoration Front. They demanded that the building be turned into a transitional shelter for those at Grove Street who were stuck there because of the dearth of affordable housing in the city. After a few hours, when the press left, the police arrived and arrested David and the student activists.

Although no one staying at the shelter was directly involved in the takeover, the initial impetus for the action clearly came from organizing meetings at the shelter. Guests and staff were involved in the planning process and attended the action as witnesses. Several local politicians were quite upset by this event and reacted by blaming the shelter staff for stirring up trouble. I heard from several sources that the mayor was quite upset by a letter I wrote, which was then sent to the local paper signed by over 20 staff and guests at the shelter, supporting the takeover and questioning her official response to the protest action.

Two weeks later, on May 1, the cot program closed for the year. I raised the question at a staff meeting a few days before about how we should respond to this event. Fifteen to twenty people were staying at the cot program on a nightly basis and would soon be without a place to stay. With the waiting list at the shelter, we could not hope to offer a bed to any of those homeless people in the next few weeks. After much discussion, we decided that the least we could do was gather tents and blankets to offer these homeless people as they waited for a bed to become available at the shelter. Donna reminded us that there was a precedent, as we had done this several times in the past, and Karen volunteered to write a public-service announcement indicating the need for these resources. All staff and administrators attended the staff meeting where this was discussed and agreed with the suggested actions. Karen then sent this request for donated tents to several of the local media. What happened next was unexpected, yet quite telling.

Local television, radio, and newspaper reporters took the request for tents that Karen had prepared for broadcast and produced a series of articles and stories suggesting that staff at the shelter were organizing a local tent city. One newspaper reporter who wanted an illustrative picture went so far as to ask Leopoldina if she would pose as a homeless person in a tent he brought. She declined the offer. A television reporter asked me on camera if I could show her where people set up tents in the city, but I explained that homeless people had been camping outside locally for a number of years. When I further explained that I would not aid her in invading these people's privacy and put them at increased risk of police harassment for illegal camping, she edited that statement out of the story and simply showed pictures of trees along the Connecticut River as a possible site of camping homeless people. Local media chose to sensationalize an exciting rumor. The coverage misled and unsettled the public.

Once again, local business leaders and politicians quickly responded to this crisis. Rather than organizing to do something about the fact that many homeless people had no safe place to sleep, they grew quite angry with shelter staff for drawing media attention to this local social problem. Several people connected with the shelter reported receiving quite explicit threats of decreased support and funding for the shelter from local business leaders and political leaders. Taking these threats quite seriously, and realizing that their own positions largely depend upon the support of these politicians, every staff person I spoke with about this reaction insisted upon anonymity beyond that provided by their names being changed in this text. The following conversation offers a representative account.

Vin: "How do you understand the reaction from various politicians to the recent takeover at the state hospital and the article about the shelter's request for tents? One person said that s/he thought these things would be tied to the shelter and the shelter would lose [the] support of downtown merchants."

Anonymous: "I think it frightens people. Radical behavior represents a loss of control and [it means] that we can't rely on people to stay in their place.... Part of staying in your place is being invisible and grateful."

"I think the three groups who allegedly reacted were the mayor, the legislatures, and the downtown business leaders. With the legislatures it embarrasses them in Boston. It looks like there's discontent among the masses out in their districts after they fought so hard to get us the money. Remember, they are the authority. It challenges them and they react like 'what, we gave them a house on the state hospital and they dare to try to take something from us.'"

"I can't tell you how many people told me that anyone who was even connected with Grove Street could [dare to] even mention tents or continue to talk about them after the actions of David and Food Not Bombs [the previous month's building takeover] was crazy. It was like, 'are you guys trying to commit organizational and funding suicide?' I never was so dramatically aware of when people give you money they own you. If you don't want to be owned, don't take money from them."

"With the mayor, it was more personal. [It was as if she said] 'I'm such an avid supporter, how could you stab me in the back by embarrassing me publicly by [engaging in behavior which can only be] implying I'm not doing enough?'"

"With the business association, again, it's a fear about tents in Pulaski Park and they are so daunted by what's going on with the young people downtown and what's happening to our city. It represents things that are out of their control. If you demand change, it invokes a fear of lack of control and loss of power and that is really frightening to people."

Although no administrators would say that it was a direct result of the actions during the spring, a few months later the shelter staff learned that our funding from the state had been decreased for the coming fiscal year. A cut of close to $30,000 represented an almost 20-per-cent decrease in total program funding. Hannah announced that staff hours would consequently have to be eliminated. This ultimately led to my voluntarily resignation from my position as Assistant Director and Leopoldina, Robert, and Karen all losing approximately four hours of paid work each week. Most significant, however, was the new awareness among remaining staff that their assigned role was clearly limited to reforming homeless people and managing homelessness if they wanted to keep their job. Consequently, the more viable "Living Wage" campaign finally getting off the ground in town had no active participation or support from any currently employed shelter staff or guests by January of 1997. A renewed focus on a program of "helping" homeless individuals through counseling and training at the shelter was emphasized by several staff and by Donald, the newly hired shelter director.

In other words, the staff were indirectly, but quite severely, reprimanded for daring to transgress the boundaries of their professional behavior. It was our professional obligation to reform homeless deviants; it was beyond the scope of our established duties to support in any way homeless protest actions or calls for a living wage. Although staff sensed this implicit prohibition all along, it took actually calling for an eradication of the conditions leading to homelessness that made the local community's prohibition an explicit one. Direct reprimands by those who publicly articulate a desire to end homelessness would have been seen as impolitic, but indirect ones could not be traced to any particular person. Those in positions of power as shelter administrators and policy makers thus retain their privileged positions while escaping blame for not favoring an end to homelessness or admitting the failure of local problem-solving efforts.

While quite exasperating to experience, these responses to the move toward oppositional activism by staff and homeless people were quite informative about additional constraints on active resistance to social inequality and homelessness. Without my activist questioning of practices and prodding for new understandings, none of these data would have emerged for me to ethnographically record. I certainly was not an impartial or objective recorder of cultural events during this research. Yet I maintain that ethnographically embodying and voicing oppositional views creates a forum for new understandings and possibilities to emerge and become visible. If I had not worked explicitly as a committed advocate for the rights of homeless people, Roberto, Ariel, David, Susan, and Raymond might well have never shared their "non-compliant" thoughts and experiences with me. Likewise, only by engaging in the type of activist work I was proposing did Ann, Gloria, and Leopoldina share their thoughts and fears about such potential practices. Only by prodding staff and guests to experiment with new practices could I uncover the depth of factors (from self-governing discursive practices to fear of lost privilege) constraining the possibilities of resistance; I also avoided the pitfalls of just another ethnography "giving voice" to, or describing behaviors of, "the homeless" but failing to analyze what produced those voices and behaviors.

Of course, an activist ethnography of everyday practices does not come without possible risks for the researcher. Although staff and guests who ventured outside their defined roles were indirectly (and, in the case of guests, sometimes quite directly) punished or threatened with loss of privilege and portrayed as "trouble-makers," I experienced similar reactions to my more activist work. As I became a more vocal critic of local policy makers through the local press, I was subtly locked out of certain meetings. While publicly claiming to agree with my analysis, shelter administrators and local policy makers began not to invite me to certain non-public meetings, for example a 1997 Mayor's forum on homelessness. There are potential consequences that come with being an activist ethnographer. If one voices oppositional views or acts in oppositional ways, one risks being portrayed as non-scholarly, unrealistic, and not a team player. Yet an engaged ethnography creates the possibility for new understandings while the "reasonable" and "realistic" daily practices remain complicit in maintaining homelessness as a normal, routine feature of life in the nation.

Through activist research, new understandings about the interconnected nature of social relations, the discursive production of subjects, the impact of socio-economic conditions, and material and discursive constraints on resistance emerge. Without my activist work, for example, my study may have been able to analyze discursive constraints on resistance practices, yet I would have remained unaware of how the desire to maintain relative material privilege and the status of being a "helping" professional also constrains staff agent reactions.

Are Alternative Resistance Strategies Possible?

After a "Living Wage Campaign" meeting one night in January 1997, Ann and I began talking about our experience with the shelter and the community. Ann had left the shelter the previous spring to concentrate on working more cooperatively with homeless people and on developing the community center. I had stopped being employed at the shelter the previous month. Both of us expressed mixed feelings of relief, exhaustion, and anguish that we were abandoning our commitments.

As Ann and I spoke, what became clear was how we had been changed by re-thinking the routine practices of the shelter industry within which we had once complicitly worked. We viewed and interacted with homeless people and sheltering experts in new ways. Ann, for example, was now friends with Ariel. Where once she was convinced that her duty was to pathologize Ariel, Ann described how much she enjoyed simply "hanging out" with her: "Ariel is just so insightful." Considering that, just two years before, Ann had become quite frustrated and angry with Ariel in her role as case manager, this was a remarkable change. Similarly, we had just come from a living wage campaign meeting where five formerly homeless people were taking leadership roles in working alongside us as friends and colleagues. That was very different than the dynamics outlined in the staff conduct policy.

Perhaps what troubled us both the most, though, was the fact that we couldn't even stop by the shelter any longer to visit because we were so disappointed in our failure to significantly alter the routine functions of the local sheltering system. Earlier that day, I had been speaking with Leopoldina in an effort to organize an educational program with the shelter and at a local community college. Leopoldina had described how the shelter had changed dramatically since we stopped working there: "It's worse than ever now. Everyone's left. [Gloria had also quit the previous spring and Donna had left in September 1996 to attend graduate school.] Staff meetings are completely horrible. We're back to censoring what people can watch on television and when they can play games. It's the old story of helping through discipline and nobody here challenges it any longer. And Donald is so happy to get rid of [troublesome homeless] people. Anyone who questions his authority in any way gets the boot."

What was perhaps most disturbing to Ann, Leopoldina, and me was how the discursive pathologization of homeless people was so deeply imbedded in the shelter and in the community. Despite our efforts during the past year, the local sheltering industry appeared to still be operating very much under a model of treating deviancy. Staff were once again urging mandatory drug testing, disclosure of bank statements, mandatory budgeting, and kicking homeless people out of the shelter for even a suspicion of drug use. Many of the small gestures that had been implemented seemed to be under attack.

By June 1997, Karen and Leopoldina were the only staff bothering to attend the weekly organizing meetings. The new director said that such work was not a vital part of his or the other staff members' jobs. Having very little staff presence made a rethinking of shelter practices quite difficult. As one guest suggested, "It's nice to sit here and talk, but what's that one hour going to do?" Additionally, Ann had recently quit the community center she helped found and had moved out of town in disgust over the direction it was taking. The objective of doing community organizing for broad-based change had been supplanted by a focus on "empowering" a select group of the more highly educated homeless people through job training, self-help, and "art therapy." This focus helped bring in a lot of money in the form of grants from the federal government, city funds, and grants from economic development foundations. Yet most homeless people in town avoided the community center at all costs. As one of the more articulate homeless people described it, "they're functioning as 'poverty pimps,' taking all that fucking money to fix us poor homeless people."

But not everything was so bleak. The dominant discourse about homelessness had been challenged with paths for discontent and organizing for social change becoming more possible. The living wage campaign started at the shelter was gaining momentum in town. "Food not Bombs" was serving food and organizing young people in town each week. The shelter newsletter (while unfortunately no longer produced or written by guests at the shelter) was being written with an emphasis on the need for living wages and affordable housing. Two ex-guests of the shelter were conducting campaigns for a seat on the city council and for mayor of Northampton. Even more telling is that when the local newspaper, the *Daily Hampshire Gazette*, interviewed candidates for the city council during the fall of 1997 three of the four questions asked by the reporter concerned the living wage campaign, the need for affordable housing, and rent control. None of these issues had been so prominent even two years previously.

One organizing meeting in late July 1997 saw approximately a dozen homeless people passionately debating how to begin working to challenge the systemic inequities that were contributing to homelessness. A significant part of this discussion focused on how to get the staff and community to stop pathologizing guests. Many of the guests and staff were quite upset at recently raised objections by a neighborhood association to the location of the winter cot program. These neighbors portrayed homeless people as lazy, mentally ill, and dangerous alcoholics. In response, Leopoldina and I, and guests at the shelter, decided to make a film for local cable access television. Shelter residents developed, shot, and edited a film whose message was that homelessness was caused by poverty and inequality and not by pathology and deviancy. Some homeless people were working collectively with some staff members in ways that previously had been unthinkable.

During that same period, I received a phone call from Raymond early one Wednesday morning about a problem at the shelter. A woman staying at the shelter had just been informed that she would have to leave the shelter because the staff suspected that she was using drugs. She reported that the shelter director had told her that she could sleep by the river and reflect on her life for seven days. If, at the end of that time, she admitted that she had a drug problem, she would be allowed to return to the shelter. However, as Raymond stated, the staff had no evidence beyond their suspicions and rumors that she was using drugs. He and I spent the remainder of that day organizing shelter guests to challenge this decision. As Raymond pointed out to Hannah, even though she was homeless she should have the right to respond to the evidence against her and not to be punished before having a chance to defend herself against false charges. Hannah eventually agreed and, after several more hours of negotiations, the woman was allowed to sleep inside again that night.

What is significant about this action is that homeless people worked together to challenge what they understood as an oppressive action. As Raymond said to me late that night, "They [the staff] thought we were power-less just because we were homeless, but I wasn't going to just stand back and see that lady sleeping on the streets for no reason. We proved to them that we have power if we act together." This is quite different than the "one man protest machine" who considered other shelter guests "just so stupid" that they couldn't see how they were being oppressed. Conceptual space had been opened in this shelter for homeless people to contemplate and voice opposi-tional beliefs. Raymond could now see some "compliant" homeless people as potential allies. Their "compliant" behavior could now be understood as a survival strategy and not only as the result of stupidity or misguided be-liefs. This new knowledge created the potential for new kinds of actions by Raymond and other homeless people.

Just as the sets of knowledge associated with the deviancy hypothesis produced certain conceptions of the homeless subject and certain actions to treat disorders, so, too, can different knowledge produce new concepts and new responses and resistances. As Ian Hacking has argued, "when new under-standings become available, when they come into circulation, or even when they become the sorts of things that it is all right to say, to think, then there are new things to choose to do. When new intentions become open to me, because new descriptions, new concepts, become available to me, I live in a new world of opportunities" (1995: 236). Such new resistance opportunities are only possible, however, when they become *conceptually* possible. For that to occur, the dominant models of charity, reform, and normalization within the shelters must be challenged.

Many residents of Northampton are quite proud of the city's reputation as a caring and compassionate community. A problem, however, remains in how local citizens continue to conceive of and "deal with" the problem of homelessness. Hundreds of caring and concerned local citizens donate money and work to provide services for "the homeless," but these efforts are based largely upon a model of normalizing or charity for deviant individuals. The very notions of emancipating the homeless and of developing a charitable community are predicated on a set of beliefs and social conditions that neces-sitate reformative practices. The significance of these institutional practices is not simply that they are largely ineffective in combatting homelessness; they also silence and partially prevent a focus on changing social inequality. By marginalizing any consideration of systemic factors, practices based upon the hegemonic "continuum of care" model serve to reinforce and maintain popular consent to homelessness while producing popular conceptions of "the homeless" in generalized categories of pathological others.

Alternatives are possible. Businesses not based on extracting surplus value from the employees could be funded with the community development block grant money. Ann, Gloria, and David have begun one small effort in that direction out of the community center. A cooperatively run coffee-grinding and wholesale business now employs a few formerly homeless individuals. Additional efforts could come from a city-wide meal tax or from having Smith College pay property taxes on the land they own. This could be used for providing affordable housing and space for cooperatively run business ventures on the grounds of the former state hospital and throughout the city. Meaningful living-wage legislation could ensure that all employees at least live above the poverty level and can afford housing. Likewise, real education and welfare reform could provide for children to be housed, raised, and educated in a more equitable fashion. Shelter staff and homeless people could work together on these efforts for social change and community organization. These are only some of the potential political implications of getting people to challenge the artificiality of the analytical categories within which their daily practices are implicated. For any of these to occur, however, the discursive conditions operating within (and outside of) the sheltering industry that make "the homeless" as a category of deviants possible need to be understood and challenged.

As long as homelessness is portrayed and discursively understood as being the result of individual shortcomings or pathologies within individual homeless people, the possibilities of resistance will continue to be constrained. Professional staff and self-blaming homeless people will continue to "fix" homeless deviancy. Homeless people will continue to engage in self-help strategies and in blaming other poor people for their economic position. Structural inequality will remain unchallenged and thought of as unalterable as long as agents are unwilling to take the risks that come with challenging those conditions. Ordinary citizens can continue to feel good about the charity work that they do while ignoring their complicity with homelessness as a social process resulting in large part from the normal, routine functioning of 1990s capitalism.

To conclude, let me return to the question of neoliberalism: how does it make sense for neoliberal policy responses to remain so dominant when they so clearly do not decrease homelessness? I am suggesting in this book that neoliberalism does work. It works to produce the systemic conditions leading to homelessness. Even more powerfully, neoliberalism works to displace attention from structural violence and onto the individualized bodies of homeless people. Neoliberalism works to produce not only homelessness within wealth, but also the rhetorical support for such conditions. If we hope to eradicate homelessness, we must counter notions that the cause of homelessness lies within individual homeless people. Instead, we must develop strategies based upon understandings of the links between homelessness, neoliberalism, transnational capital, and an increasingly global war on poor people. Not to do so allows the structural violence of which homelessness is simply one outcome to continue. A "caring," "helping" community engaged in "reasonable" helping efforts and charitable work, even in the "most enlightened" city in Massachusetts, is not the answer if we hope to see an end to homelessness.

References

Albelda, Randy, Nancy Folbre, and the Center for Popular Economics. 1996. *The War on the Poor*. New York: New Press.

Anderson, Mark. 1996. "Social Justice: An Interview with Kip Tiernan." *Z Magazine* 5: 41–46.

Bassuk, Ellen. 1984. "Is Homelessness a Mental Health Problem?" *American Journal of Psychiatry* 41(12): 1546–49.

Bernstein, Jared, Elizabeth McNichol, Lawrence Mishel, and Robert Zahradnik. 2000. *Pulling Apart: A State by State Analysis of Income Trends*. Washington, DC: Center on Budget and Policy Priorities and Economic Policy Institute.

Blau, Joel. 1992. *The Visible Poor: Homelessness in the United States*. New York: Oxford University Press.

Bourgois, Phillipe. 1995. *In Search of Respect: Selling Crack in El Barrio*. Cambridge: Cambridge University Press.

Brown, Judson. 2000. "Basic Needs Go Unmet for Many." *Daily Hampshire Gazette* 18 Jan: 1.

Burchell, Graham. 1996. "Liberal Government and Techniques of the Self." In *Foucault and Political Reason: Liberalism, Neo-Liberalism, and Rationalities of Government*. Ed. Andrew Barry, Thomas Osborne, and Nikolas Rose. Chicago: University of Chicago Press.

Burt, Martha. 1992. *Over the Edge: The Growth of Homelessness in the 1980s*. Washington, DC: The Urban Institute Press.

Burt, Martha. 1997. "Causes of the Growth of Homelessness during the 1980s." In *Understanding Homelessness: New Policy and Research Perspectives*. Washington, DC: Fannie Mae Foundation.

Center on Budget and Policy Priorities. 1994. *1993 Poverty and Income Trends*. Washington, DC: Center on Budget and Policy Priorities.

Comaroff, John, and Jean Comaroff. 1991. *Of Revelation and Revolution: Christianity, Colonialism, and Consciousness in South Africa*. Vol. 1. Chicago: The University of Chicago Press.

Connolly, Deb. 2000. *Homeless Mothers*. Minneapolis: University of Minnesota Press.

Cruikshank, Barbara. 1994. "The Will to Empower: Technologies of Citizenship and the War on Poverty." *Socialist Review* 23: 29–55.

Cruikshank, Barbara. 1996. "Revolutions Within: Self Government and Self Esteem" In *Foucault and Political Reason: Liberalism, Neo-Liberalism, and Rationalities of Government*. Ed. Andrew Barry, Thomas Osborne, and Nikolas Rose. Chicago: University of Chicago Press.

Davidson, Pem Buck. 2001. "Worked to the Bone: Race, Class, Power and Privilege in Kentucky." New York: Monthly Review Press.

Davis, Dana-Ain. 2003. "What Did You Do Today?: Notes from a Politically Engaged Anthropologist." *Urban Anthropology and Studies of Cultural Systems and World Economic Development* 32(2): 147–76.

de Certeau, Michel. 1984. *The Practice of Everyday Life*. Trans. S. F. Rendall. Berkeley: University of California Press.

Dehavenon, Anna Lou. 1993. *Out of Sight! Out of Mind! or, How New York City and New York State Tried to Abandon the City's Homeless Families in 1993*. New York: The Action Research Project on Hunger, Homelessness and Family Health.

Dehavenon, Anna Lou (ed.). 1996. *There's No Place Like Home: Anthropological Perspectives on Housing and Homelessness in the United States*. Westport: Bergin & Garvey.

Demartino, George. 1999. *Global Economy, Global Justice: Theoretical Objections and Policy Alternatives to Neoliberalism*. London: Routledge.

DeParle, Jason. 1996. "Slamming the Door." *The New York Times Magazine* 20 Oct.: 52–95.

Desjarlais, Robert. 1997. *Shelter Blues: Sanity and Sainthood Among the Homeless*. Philadelphia: University of Pennsylvania Press.

Dolbeare, Cushing. 1999. *Out of Reach: The Gap Between Housing Costs and Income of Poor People in the United States*. Washington, DC: National Low Income Housing Coalition.

Dordick, Gwendolyn. 1997. *Something Left to Lose: Personal Relations and Survival among New York's Homeless*. Philadelphia: Temple University Press.

Egan, Timothy. 1993. "In 3 Progressive Cities, Stern Homeless Policies." *The New York Times* 12 Dec.: 26.

Elliot, Marta, and Lauren Krivo. 1991. "Structural Determinants of Homelessness in the United States." *Social Problems* 38(1): 113–32.

Farmer, Paul. 2003. *Pathologies of Power: Health, Human Rights, and the New War on the Poor*. Berkeley: University of California Press.

Foucault, Michel. 1979. *Discipline & Punish: The Birth of the Prison*. New York: Vintage Books.

Foucault, Michel. 1991. *Remarx on Marx: Conversations with Duccio Trombadori*. New York: Semiotext(e).

Fox Piven, Frances, Joan Acker, Margaret Hallock, and Sandra Morgen. 2002. *Work, Welfare, and Politics: Confronting Poverty in the Wake of Welfare Reform.* Eugene: University of Oregon Press.

Friedman, Leon. 1997. "Downsizing the Deficit? It's Time the Very Rich Paid Their Fair Share: A Snare-the-Wealth Tax." *The Nation* 6 Jan.: 23–23.

Gans, Herbert. 1995. *The War Against the Poor: The Underclass and AntiPoverty Policy.* New York: Basic Books.

Gibson, Timothy. 1998. "I Don't Want Them Living Around Here: Ideologies of Race and Neighborhood Decay." *Rethinking Marxism* 10(4): 141–55.

Goode, Judith, and Jeff Maskovsky. 2001. *The New Poverty Studies: The Ethnography of Power, Politics and Impoverished People in the United States.* New York: New York University Press.

Gounis, Kostas 1992. "The Manufacture of Dependency: Shelterization Revisited." *New England Journal of Public Policy* 8(1): 685–93.

Gregory, Steven. 1998. *Black Corona: Race and the Politics of Place in an Urban Community.* Princeton: Princeton University Press.

Gupta, Akhil, and James Ferguson. 1997. *Anthropological Locations: Boundaries and Grounds of a Field Science.* Berkeley: University of California Press.

Hacking, Ian. 1986. "Making Up People." In *Reconstructing Individualism: Autonomy, Individualism, and the Self in Western Thought.* Ed. Thomas Heller, Morton Sosna, and David Wellbery. Stanford: Stanford University Press.

Hacking, Ian. 1991. "How Should We Do the History of Statistics?" In *The Foucault Effect: Studies in Governmentality.* Ed. Graham Burchell, Colin Gordon, and Peter Miller. Hemel Hempstead: Harvester Wheatsheaf.

Hacking, Ian. 1995. *Rewriting the Soul: Multiple Personality Disorder and the Science of Memory.* Princeton: Princeton University Press.

Hall, Stuart. 1988a. "The Toad in the Garden: Thatcherism among the Theorists." In *Marxism and the Interpretation of Culture.* Ed. Cary Nelson and Lawrence Grossberg. Urbana and Chicago: University of Illinois Press.

Hall, Stuart. 1988b. *The Hard Road to Renewal: Thatcherism and the Crisis of the Left.* London and New York: Verso.

Harrison, Faye. 1997. *Decolonizing Anthropology: Moving Further Toward an Anthropology for Liberation.* 2nd ed. Arlington, VA: Association of Black Anthropologists and American Anthropological Association.

Hopper, Kim. 1988. "More than Passing Strange: Homelessness and Mental Illness in New York City." *American Ethnologist* 15(1): 155–67.

Hopper, Kim, Ezra Susser, and Sarah Conover. 1985. "Economics of Makeshift: Deindustrialization and Homelessness in New York City." *Urban Anthropology* 14(1): 183–235.

Horn, Patricia, and Randy Albelda. 1992. "Justice, Not Charity: Activist Kip Tiernan Confronts the Homeless Shelter Industry." *Dollars & Sense* September: 12–13.

Hyatt, Susan Brin. 1995. "Poverty and Difference: Ethnographic Representations of 'Race' and the Crisis of 'the Social.'" In *Gender and Race Through Education and Political Activism: The Legacy of Sylvia Helen Forman*. Ed. Dena Shenk. Washington, DC: American Anthropological Association/Association for Feminist Anthropology.

Hyatt, Susan Brin. 1997. "Poverty in a 'Post-Social' Landscape: Tenant Management Policies, Self-Governance, and the Democratization of Knowledge in Great Britain." In *The Anthropology of Policy*. Ed. Sue Wright and Chris Shore. London: Routledge Press.

Interagency Council on the Homeless. 1999. *The Forgotten Americans —Homelessness: Programs and the People They Serve*. Washington, DC: United States Department of Housing and Urban Development.

Jencks, Christopher. 1994. *The Homeless*. Cambridge, MA: Harvard University Press.

Kaufman, Trace. 1997. *Out of Reach: Rental Housing at What Cost?* Washington, DC: National Low Income Housing Coalition.

Kelley, Robin. 1997. *Yo' Mama's Disfunktional! Fighting the Culture Wars in Urban America*. Boston: Beacon Press.

Kidder, Tracey. 1999. *Hometown*. New York: Random House

Kim, Jim Yong, Joyce Millen, Alec Irwin, and John Gershman. 2000. *Dying for Growth: Global Inequality and the Health of the Poor*. Monroe, ME: Common Courage Press.

Kozol, Jonathan. 1991. *Savage Inequalities: Children in America's Schools*. New York: Crown Publishers.

Kozol, Jonathan. 1995. *Amazing Grace: The Lives of Children and the Conscience of a Nation*. New York: Crown Publishers.

Kraker, Daniel, and Jay Walljasper. 1997. "The Most Enlightened Town in Every State." *Utne Reader* 6 May: 58.

Lav, Iris J., and Edward Lazere. 1996. *A Hand Up: How State Earned Income Credits Help Working Families Escape Poverty, 1996 Edition*. Washington, DC: Center on Budget and Policy Priorites.

Laws, Glenda. 1996. "Geography and Social Justice." *Annals of the Association of American Geographers* 86(2): 390–412.

Lazere, Edward. 1995. *In Short Supply: The Growing Affordable Housing Gap*. Washington, DC: Center on Budget and Policy Priorities.

Liebow, Elliot. 1993. *Tell Them Who I Am: The Lives of Homeless Women*. New York: The Free Press.

Lock, Margaret, and Nancy Scheper-Hughes. 1990. "A Critical-Interpretive Approach in Medical Anthropology: Rituals and Routines of Discipline and Dissent." In *Medical Anthropology: Contemporary Theory and Methods*. Ed. Thomas M. Johnson and Carolyn F. Sargent. New York: Praeger Books.

Lyon-Callo, Vincent. 1998. "Constraining Responses to Homelessness: An Ethnographic Exploration of the Impact of Funding Concerns on Resistance." *Human Organization* 57(1): 1–8.

Lyon-Callo, Vincent. 2000. "Medicalizing Homelessness: The Production of Self-Blame and Self-Governing within Homeless Shelters." *Medical Anthropology Quarterly* 14(3): 328–45.

Lyon-Callo, Vincent. 2001. "Making Sense of NIMBY: Poverty, Power, and Community Opposition to Homeless Shelters." *City & Society* xiii(2): 183–209.

Marcuse, Peter. 1989. "Gentrification, Homelessness, and the Work Process." *Housing Studies* 4: 211–20.

Market Street Research. 1994. *Health and Human Service Needs of Hampshire County Residents: Needs Assessment Report*. Northampton, MA: Market Street Research, Inc.

Massachusetts Institute for Social and Economic Research. 1990. 1990 Census of Population and Housing, Summary Tape File 3: Northampton. Amherst, MA: Massachusetts Institute for Social and Economic Research

Mathieu, Arline. 1993. "The Medicalization of Homelessness and the Theater of Repression." *Medical Anthropology Quarterly* 7(2): 170–84.

McNichol, Tom. 1995. "Caring Has Its Limits: More Cities are Passing Tough Anti-homeless Measures as 'Compassion Fatigue' Sets In." *USA Weekend* 6–8 Jan.: 8.

National Coalition for the Homeless. 1997. *Homelessness in America: Unabated and Increasing*. Washington, DC: National Coalition for the Homeless.

National Coalition for the Homeless. 2003. *People Need Affordable Housing*. Washington, DC: National Coalition for the Homeless.

National Law Center on Homelessness and Poverty. 1997. *Access Delayed, Access Denied: Local Opposition to Housing and Services for Homeless People Across the United States*. Washington, DC: National Law Center on Homelessness and Poverty.

National Law Center on Homelessness and Poverty. 1999. *Out of Sight   Out of Mind? A Report on Anti-Homeless Laws, Litigation, and Alternatives in 50 United States Cities*. Washington, DC: National Law Center on Homelessness and Poverty.

National Priorities Project. 1999. *Working Hard, Earning Less: The Story of Job Growth in Massachusetts*. Northampton, MA: National Priorities Project.

Navarro, Vicente. 1986. *Crisis, Health, and Medicine: A Social Critique*. New York: Tavistock Publishers.

Navarro, Vicente. 2000. *The Political Economy of Social Inequalities: Consequences for Health and Quality of Life*. Amityville, NY: Baywood Publishing Company.

O'Flaherty, Brendan. 1996. *Making Room: The Economics of Homelessness*. Cambridge: Cambridge University Press.

Rabinow, Paul. 1989. *French Modern: Norms and Forms of the Social Environment*. Cambridge, MA: The MIT Press.

Resnick, Stephen, and Richard Wolff. 1987. *Knowledge and Class: A Marxian Critique of Political Economy*. Chicago: University of Chicago Press.

Rodriguez, Cheryl. 2003. "Invoking Fannie Lou Hamer: Research, Ethnography, and Activism in Low Income Communities." *Urban Anthropology and Studies of Cultural Systems and World Economic Development* 32(2): 231–51.

Rose, Nikolas. 1991. "Governing by Numbers." *Accounting, Organization, and Society* 16(7): 673–92.

Rose, Nikolas. 1994. "Expertise and the Government of Conduct." *Studies in Law, Politics and Society* 14: 359–367.

Rose, Nikolas. 1996a. *Inventing Our Selves: Psychology, Power and Personhood*. Cambridge: Cambridge University Press.

Rose, Nikolas. 1996b. "Governing 'Advanced' Liberal Democracies." In *Foucault and Political Reason: Liberalism, Neo-Liberalism and Rationalities of Government*. Ed. Andrew Barry, Thomas Osborne, and Nikolas Rose. Chicago: University of Chicago Press.

Rose, Nikolas. 1996c. "The Death of the Social? Re-Figuring the Territories of Government." *Economy and Society* 25(3): 327–56.

Ruddick, Susan. 1995. *Young and Homeless in Hollywood: Mapping Social Identities*. London: Routledge.

Rutheisser, Charles. 1996. *Imagineering Atlanta: The Politics of Place in the City of Dreams*. London: Verso.

Schensul, Stephen, and Jean J. Schensul. 1978. "Advocacy and Applied Anthropology." *Social Scientists as Advocates*. Ed. George Weber and George McCall. Beverly Hills, CA: Sage.

Scheper-Hughes, Nancy. 1992. *Death Without Weeping: The Violence of Everyday Life in Brazil*. Berkeley: University of California Press.

Scheper-Hughes, Nancy. 1995. "The Primacy of the Ethical: Propositions for a Militant Anthropology." *Current Anthropology* 36(3): 409–20.

Scott, James. 1990. *Domination and the Arts of Resistance: Hidden Transcripts.* New Haven, CT: Yale University Press.

Singer, Merrill. 1990. "Another Perspective on Advocacy." *Current Anthropology* 31(5): 548–49.

Singer, Merrill, Freddie Valentin, Hans Baer, and Zhongke Jia. 1992. "Why Does Juan Garcia Have a Drinking Problem?" *Medical Anthropology* 14(1): 77–108.

Spain, James, and Robert Talbott. 1996. *Hoover's Handbook of American Businesses, 1996.* Austin: The Reference Press.

Spivak, Gayatri. "Can the Subaltern Speak?" In *Marxism and the Interpretation of Cultures.* Ed. Cary Nelson and Lawrence Grossberg. Urbana and Chicago: University of Illinois Press.

Stiglitz, Joseph. 2002. *Globalization and Its Discontents.* New York: W.W. Norton.

Susser, Ida. 1982. *Norman Street: Poverty and Politics in an Urban Neighborhood.* New York: Oxford University Press.

Takahashi, Lois. 1998. *Homelessness, AIDS, and Stigmitization: The NIMBY Syndrome in the United States at the end of the Twentieth Century.* Oxford: Clarendon Press.

United States Bureau of the Census. 1996. *Poverty in the United States: 1995.* Washington, DC: US Bureau of the Census.

United States Conference of Mayors. 1998. *A Status Report on Hunger and Homelessness in America's Cities: 1988.* Washington, DC: United States Conference of Mayors.

United States Department of Health and Human Services. 2003. *Ending Chronic Homelessness: Strategies for Action.* Washington, DC: Department of Health and Human Services.

United States Department of Housing and Urban Development. 2000. *Rental Housing Assistance — The Worsening Crisis: A Report to Congress on Worst Case Housing Needs.* Washington, DC: Office of Policy Development and Research.

Urla, Jaqueline. 1993. "Cultural Politics in an Age of Statistics: Numbers, Nations and the Making of Basque Identity." *American Ethnologist* 20(4): 818–843.

Watson, Bruce. 1996. "Tight Rental Market Aggravates Annual Housing Scramble." *Daily Hampshire Gazette* 28 Aug.: 15–16.

Waxman, Laura, and Sharon Hinderliter. 1995. *A Status Report on Hunger and Homelessness in America's Cities: 1996.* Washington, DC: US Conference of Mayors.

Williams, Brett. 1996. "There Goes the Neighborhood: Gentrification, Displacement, and Homelessness in Washington D.C." In *There's No Place*

Like Home:Anthropological Perspectives on Housing and Homelessness in the United States. Ed. Anna Lou Dehavenon. Westport: Bergin and Garvey.

Williams, Raymond. 1977. *Marxism and Literature*. Oxford: Oxford University Press.

Wolch, Jennifer, and Michael Dear. 1993. *Malign Neglect: Homelessness in an American City*. San Francisco: Jossey-Bass Publishers.

Wright, Talmadge, 1997. *Out of Place: Homeless Mobilizations, Subcities, and Contested Landscapes*. Albany: State University of New York Press.

Young, Alan. 1995. *The Harmony of Illusions: Inventing Post Traumatic Stress Disorder*. Princeton: Princeton University Press.

Young, Alan. 1982. "The Anthropologies of Illness and Sickness" *Annual Review of Anthropology* 11: 257–85.

Index